THE
REVELATION
EPIC

PREPARING YOUTH GROUPS FOR THE EARTH'S FINAL DAYS

A Creative Study of Revelation 5-22

THE REVELATION EPIC

PREPARING YOUTH GROUPS FOR THE EARTH'S FINAL DAYS

David Olshine

EMPOWERED® Youth Products
Standard Publishing
Cincinnati, Ohio

IN MEMORY OF MRS. PAT BRADLEY (1939-2001)

Pat Bradley, affectionately known by our students as "Momma Pat," faithfully served in our youth ministries department for six years as my secretary, administrative assistant, confidante and friend. Our staff and students miss her greatly. "Mrs. B." is now experiencing what Revelation is all about, worshiping the Lamb of God around the throne.

CONTENTS

All Scripture quotations, unless otherwise indicated, are taken from the *Holy Bible*, New Living Translation, copyright © 1996. Used by permission of Tyndale House Publishers, Inc., Wheaton, Illinois 60189. All rights reserved.

Scripture quotations marked THE MESSAGE are taken from *The Message*, copyright © by Eugene H. Peterson, 1993, 1994, 1995. Used by permission of NavPress Publishing Group.

Edited by Dale Reeves and Patricia Senseman
Cover design by Ahaa! Design
Inside design by Dina Sorn

Standard Publishing, Cincinnati, Ohio. A Division of Standex International Corporation.

10 09 08 07 06 05 04 03

5 4 3 2 1

ISBN: 0-7847-1301-4

HOW TO USE THIS BOOK

Acknowledgments

Dedicated to my first three mentors. Thanks for your impact and influence on my life.
- To Joe Bishman, my first pastor. You taught me to never be afraid of the book of Revelation.
- To Mark Rowland, peer, colleague and role model. You helped me discern my future with prayer, loving confrontation and humor (and in the process I discovered my calling and my wife!).
- To Michael Slaughter, through word and deed, you showed me the power of vision and commitment. You modeled how to "dream dreams" and never give up!

Special Thanks

- To F. Dale "Dunk" Reeves, my fabulous editor and friend. Thanks for the vision for this curriculum and your Empowered® team.
- To those student ministries that allowed us to field test *The Revelation Epic*: Cornerstone Presbyterian; Spring Valley Baptist Church; Trinity Baptist; The Minnesota United Methodist Senior High Youth Conference; Fellowship of Christian Athletes; Northside Baptist Church; First Nazarene; and Kingsland United Methodist Church.
- To my wife Rhonda, and children Rachel and Andrew. You make life overflowing for me.

In the first elective study called *The Revelation Letters*, I dealt with the first four chapters of Revelation. Revelation means "unveiling" and the entire book points to the unveiling of Jesus Christ. The first four chapters focus on Jesus' words to seven churches as they prepared for the return of Christ.

The Revelation Epic covers chapters 5-22, and here we have a glimpse of visions for the earth's final days. These chapters describe the emergence of the beast and his mark, the return of Jesus as the conquering warrior and the awesome picture of Heaven where believers stand to worship their King. There's so much symbolism, imagery and theology wrapped up in Revelation that one or two books simply cannot capture everything. This study addresses the major themes your students need to consider.

Each session in this course has a plan for your success as a leader. Here's a quick breakdown of how each study is laid out:

Opening Shakes are *openers* designed to get your students interested and involved in the session. I've included a variety of experience-oriented activities that use either group work, music, stories or other media.

Book Quakes is the section that provides the bulk of biblical insights. It consists of a brief Scripture commentary you can use as you teach the session. Consider reading these sections ahead of time, and sprinkling the information throughout your teaching time.

Teaching Tremors will allow your students to interact with the truths in Revelation. Each session uses reproducible student sheets and several interactive-learning experiences to help your group engage the Word.

Controversial Q and A entries tackle some of the more difficult questions that arise from a study of the book of Revelation. I've included these for you to use in your teaching, or to prepare you for some of the more difficult questions students might throw at you.

Aftershocks contain extra teaching options to spice up your teaching and additional resources to help you in your study.

Cosmic Closures give your students the opportunity to live out the particular truth addressed in the session in a way that's real and applicable to their lives.

What's Up With That? sidebars explain some of the most interesting concepts of Revelation.

Media Moments connect teens with various contemporary songs, video/DVD clips and other sources of media. Make sure you explain the background of the song or clip before you press "play." These sidebars include music or movie clip suggestions that reinforce the teaching of the day. WARNING! Preview all film clips before using them. They are not always obviously "spiritual" or self-explanatory. Weave these illustrations into your presentation of the material.

Without proper explanation before or after, they might become simply entertainment and not a powerful teaching tool. Also, there could possibly be offensive material before or after the suggested clip, so know when to start and stop it. These choices have been selected with a perspective of "bridging the gap" with unchurched teens and "seekers" with little or no church background. NOTE: The start points noted are from the opening studio logo of the movie, not the beginning of your tape. Reset the counter to 0:00:00 when the studio logo appears.

PREPARING TO TEACH

If you've worked with students for a while, you already know that it's almost impossible to completely prepare for a Bible study. You never know if an activity will work, you're never quite certain what questions students will ask and you never know what the Holy Spirit will do in the middle of, or after a study.

Preparing to teach, however, is much more about our vision for learning than it is about preparing a lesson. Simply put—if we have a vision for learning, then our lesson preparation is more focused, more complete, and in the end, will be more life-changing.

With that in mind, take a few minutes and read through the following seven "visions for teaching" points listed below. After each point, consider the corresponding question, then take some time to reflect on your vision for your students, and how they live out God's Word.

I HAVE A VISION FOR DISCUSSION, NOT LECTURE.
The best communicators to students learn how to *facilitate* discussions. Oftentimes, we learn how to do this by first making mistakes on how not to teach. A 20-minute lecture might be acceptable in some places, but it isn't the best model for youth ministry. Spend time drawing your students "out," so that they do not turn "in" and withdraw. The goal is to engage students, not alienate them. Typically, lecture turns youth off, especially when it comes to spiritual things. Sermonizing leads teens frequently to "disengage." Discussion, on the other hand, is inclusive and empowers students to know that their ideas matter.
Question: Do your students feel that their ideas really count?

II HAVE A VISION FOR TRANSFORMATION, NOT JUST INFORMATION.
The book of Revelation has many wild and weird images. The concepts are often difficult to grasp, even for people who study this book on a regular basis. Information is necessary, but information alone will create tension for you and your students. Information without application will lead to frustration. *But, information with application will lead to transformation.* Your ultimate goal as a teacher of God's Word is to see change in the lives of your students.
Question: Do you see yourself primarily as a dispenser of information, or as an agent of God to bring about changed lives for Christ?

III HAVE A VISION TO KEEP THE SESSION ACTIVE, NOT PASSIVE.
The common complaint by many teens in Sunday school and youth group is "BORING." Why? My "take" is that we have made it too passive. I personally believe that too often we teachers do all of

the hard work. We try and entertain. We seek to impress. We share *our* insights. And meanwhile, we allow our students to sit restless until the time is over. Catch a vision that active is better than passive. Keep things hopping!

Question: Is learning operating at an active or passive level with your group?

IV HAVE A VISION TO REMAIN FAITHFUL TO THE SCRIPTURE.

Your challenge as a teacher, especially with Revelation, is not to give in to theories, speculations and preposterous notions about the "end of the world." The best way to interpret Scripture is simple: *always line up Scripture with Scripture.* What was the author's original intent when he wrote the words to the audience of his day? How are we to interpret the meanings? How are we to apply it today?

Question: Do you keep the Bible as central in your teaching?

V HAVE A VISION FOR "LESS IS MORE."

Too often our classes, small groups and youth meetings merely present a smorgasbord of facts and trivia. Too much information can be a turnoff. Teens need simple concepts that they can "take home and still remember later." These sessions in *The Revelation Epic* are designed to be 30-40 minutes in length, so don't try using every option! Remember that "less is more."

Question: Are you overloading your students with too much information?

VI HAVE A VISION FOR UNDERSTANDING THE DIFFERENT LEARNING STYLES OF YOUTH.

Consider these four styles of learning. Ben is an *innovative* learner. He loves discussion and small groups. Ben enjoys creativity and innovation. Jennifer is an *analytical* learner and takes in knowledge by watching, listening and observing. Jennifer learns as she takes notes, for she engages with an auditory style. Mark's way to understand data is through *common sense*. Mark doesn't really care about theory ("why"), he wants to know "how" something works. Common-sense learners need to ask questions and receive practical answers. Questions leave lasting impressions. Sometimes questions actually are better than answers! Tiffany is a *dynamic* learner and needs to experience life. Dynamic learners are risk takers. They "do" life through experimentation.

The truth is, we teach like we learn. Our job as educators is to *know* our students' learning styles, and then *teach* to all of them. If we teach only to students who learn like us, then we'll miss the majority of our students.

Question: How well do you know your students' styles of learning?

VII HAVE A VISION FOR CREATIVE TEAM TEACHING.

Don't try to teach alone. Find some others to help facilitate the time with you. Utilize other adults and students. Creativity seems to "beget" creativity. When we try and teach individually, our ideas run dry quickly. The Lone Ranger needed Tonto, Laurel needed Hardy and you need a helper. A two-hour weekly brainstorming session with a co-leader will pay off huge dividends and your sessions will stay alive and fresh.

Question: What steps do you need to take to have a team mentality?

After asking yourself these seven questions, take a moment to think back through your answers. What areas do you feel you might want to work through so you can be more effective in your teaching? In what areas are you awesome, and think you need to celebrate a little? Reflect for a moment, and remember that no leader is perfect—we're all clay in God's hands for His sake, and for the students he's given us to teach.

After you've reflected, and as you prepare to teach these sessions, remember this: God has called you to be an E.P.I.C. teacher. He's given you students to mold. He's called you to be his EPIC hands and feet for students. What do I mean by EPIC?

E-Experiential

While I've designed each session to be experiential so students can fully understand God at work in Revelation, it's your job to bring them to life. Do your best to make these sessions leap off the paper. Make them exciting. Kick these sessions around, and create new ways for students to get inside the ideas.

P-Participation

I had a volunteer tell me once, "I am getting more out of the teaching than the students!" (This was true—he talked all the time, and never let students get involved). If we're not letting students engage the material, we're totally missing the mark. Let them participate! Encourage discussion, small groups, skits and anything else that makes you close your mouth, and causes them to talk to you, and each other.

I-Inclusive

Every student that takes the time to attend your sessions (whether they want to be there or not), has the right and privilege to be involved. From week to week you may not know who's going to show up. On any given night you could have a mixture of jocks, introverts, geeks and prom queens. It's your job to include all of these students. Find ways to include the introvert, the troubled, the bored, the know-it-all or the one who knows nothing. Make your sessions inclusive.

C-Care

The axiom is true, "Teens don't care how much we know until they know how much we (adults) care." The sessions may be experiential, participatory and inclusive, but if your students do not feel that you are interested in their lives, Christian community will be absent. Jesus told us the mark of the Christian is to "love one another." Make it your heart's goal and prayer to love your teens deeply.

Have a great time with your teens with this study. My prayer is that you and your students will be changed through the Word of God. Let *The Revelation Epic* begin!

Blessings,
David Olshine

INTRODUCTION to Revelation

WHO WROTE THE BOOK?

The apostle John on the island of Patmos wrote the book of Revelation. John was the disciple of Jesus who also wrote the Gospel of John, 1, 2, 3 John and of course, Revelation. Five times the author identifies himself as John (1:1, 2, 4, 9; 22:8). This is the same John who is referred to as "the beloved disciple" of Jesus. John was the only disciple to die at an old age; all the rest were martyred for their faith.

WHEN WAS IT WRITTEN?

The book was written during a time of intense persecution, probably during the time of Emperor Domitian, somewhere between A.D. 90-95. John was being "silenced" by the emperor because of his strong Christian faith and was exiled to the island of Patmos (west of modern-day Turkey in the Aegean Sea).

WHY WAS IT WRITTEN?

During John's time on Patmos, he received a vision from Jesus. Many of God's people had visions: Daniel, Ezekiel, Jeremiah, Peter and Paul, to name a few. These visions came to John through an angel. In this study we are taking some liberties at addressing youth groups specifically, even though the original intent was not aimed at 21st-century churches. The Bible as God's Word penetrates all cultures and all times and seasons. The events of the past few years have caused some anxiety about the future in the minds of today's young adults. Teens today have many questions. As you crack open the book, the truth will come to light, questions will be answered and lives will be changed. Hang on, it's sure to be a wild ride.

A SEAL STORY

The opening scene takes place in Heaven. On the center stage stands a throne. Seated on the throne is a lamb that has been slain. Why a lamb? A lamb was the sacrifice for humanity's sinfulness. Who is this lamb? The Lamb is the Lord Jesus Christ. Everything is focused on the throne, and on the Lamb. What's happening? Unceasing worship of the Lamb of God! While millions are bowing before the Lamb, he begins breaking open seals and unrolling scrolls. The first scroll holds God's judgment. And, when the Lamb opens it, God's judgment is released on the earth. His judgment divided the faithful from the unfaithful. In the end, no one questions that "Salvation comes from our God on the throne and from the Lamb!" (7:10).

OPENING SHAKES

I MAN ON THE STREET

Before your meeting, grab a video camera and hit the streets. Ask some people (preferably teenagers) the question, "What does the word 'worship' mean to you?" Tell them there are no boundaries to the question, no right or wrong response. Once you have several interviews, get someone to splice it together for you.

Show this as an opener, explaining to your students, **"We headed out into the community to see what people think of when they hear the word 'worship.' Here is what we discovered."**

After they view the video, allow students to respond to these questions:
- **Is there one right way to worship Jesus?**
- **Is there one kind of worship music that's the best?**
- **Define the word "worship."**

Wrap up the opener by saying something like, **"Worshiping God is awesome. You've heard a lot of different opinions about what worship is. Let's see what the Bible says about how believers will be worshiping God at the end of time."**

II GUESS THE ROTTING FOOD

Way before the meeting you'll need to get some food and help it rot a little. You might want to put some ground beef outside for a few days, allow milk to spoil, etc. If you have trouble getting your hands on rotting food, you might want to consider just putting several smelly foods (like fish or cheese) together. Put each food in a separate container. Place the food containers in a row on a table at one end of the room.

After all students have arrived, divide them into two groups and ask groups to gather at the opposite side of the room away from the rotting food. Begin by asking, **"Have you ever opened something in**

LESSON TEXT
REVELATION 5:1–7:17

LESSON FOCUS
Jesus Christ, the Lamb of God, is worthy to be worshiped because he overcame sin and death.

LESSON GOALS
As a result of participating in this session, students will:
- Learn of Heaven's theme— an eternity spent worshiping the Lamb of God.
- Discover the meaning of the scroll and the unleashing of the seals.
- Understand tribulation, a cosmic earthquake and God's protective power.

Materials needed:
Video cameras; blank videotapes; TV and VCR

AFTERSHOCKS

If you've got a group of students that need to be mobile, give them video cameras, tape recorders, or just pens and papers and ask *them* to interview a few people and get their responses about what worship is. Allow students a few minutes to do this. When groups return, have them share their group's interview. This is an oldie, but it will help your students firmly grasp the variety of thoughts about worship.

Materials needed:
Rotting food; containers; a table; two blindfolds

Media Moment

Play the song "I Can Only Imagine" by MercyMe. It is recorded on their *Almost There* CD. This song will help your students contemplate a little bit about what it's like to worship God in Heaven. "The Heart of Worship," by Matt Redman is an outstanding tune related to worship. It can be found on various albums by Matt Redman and on several WorshipTogether compilations.

the refrigerator, and it was so awful that you nearly tossed your cookies? Today you're going to have the chance to guess the identity of some rotten foods."

Give each group one blindfold, and ask each of them to blindfold one person from their group. Ask each blindfolded person to come forward and take the lid off one of the containers. Blindfolded students must guess what the food is that they smell. Give each student a chance to guess.

Conclude this activity by explaining, **"Sometimes when you open a container you're not sure what will happen. Today we're going to look at a part of Revelation in which the apostle John witnesses scrolls being opened, and some incredible worship is the result."**

BOOK QUAKES

REVELATION 5:1-14

The scene is Heaven. The focus is the scroll, which was a document or contract written on papyrus. It was about eight inches wide and ten inches long. It contained a will that often included a deed, similar to a marriage license. This will was sealed with seven seals. The Romans sealed their seals seven times to prevent unlawful entry. A "strong angel" wanted to know who could open the scroll. The author and witness of this "revelation," John began to weep because he didn't think anyone could open the scroll.

One of the 24 elders around the throne told John to stop crying because "the Lion of the tribe of Judah" had won! The term "Lion of Judah" was a reference from Genesis 49:8-10, a prophecy of the coming Messiah. Lions are animals of great strength, and Jesus, the God-man, is of great potency and influence. Jesus came from the ancestry of "the root of David," clearly another messianic title (see Isaiah 11:1-10).

Then John looked and saw a Lamb with seven horns, symbolizing that Jesus has complete power over all humanity. The Lamb has absolute authority, and Heaven is captured by his presence. The 24 elders fell down before the Lamb and the four living beings worshiped him. At the heart of Heaven is Jesus—and people are standing around him, worshiping him day and night. Millions of angels are around the throne worshiping Jesus. All of Heaven and earth are declaring his glory.

6:1-11

In chapter five, Jesus was the only one worthy to open the scroll. In chapter six, Christ breaks the seals. The first seal revealed a white horse, and its rider carried a bow. A crown was on his head. The next set of seals were unleashed on the earth: war represented by a red horse; famine characterized by a black horse; massive death was depicted as a horse with a pale green color, ashen—like that of a corpse. During the opening of this fourth seal twenty-five percent of the world's population died. The fifth seal was opened, and John saw believers in Christ who had been "martyred" for their faith. A martyr means "to witness." These were men and women who had an experiential relationship with Jesus and died for their faith. And they were each rewarded with a white robe.

6:12-17

The sixth seal was broken and it set off a great earthquake. The sun became black, the moon blood red and the stars of the sky fell—the sky itself even went away! All of the mountains and islands on earth disappeared. With all this calamity and tragedy upon the earth, you'd think that people would plead to God for deliverance. The martyrs cried out, "Avenge us"; whereas the rest cried out, "Fall on us and hide us from the face of the one who sits on the throne and from the wrath of the Lamb." In his work, *E-Quake: Unlocking the Book of Revelation*, Jack Hayford believes that chapters six and 16 of Revelation are the exact same events "seen from two different perspectives." Hayford believes that this earth-wide impact is a "cosmic event" (p. 169). (See "Resources for Revelation" on page 63.) This chapter ends by asking the question, "Who will survive?"

7:1-13

Four angels stood at the four corners of the earth holding back the four winds from blowing. These four angels had power to injure the land and sea. Another angel appeared, carrying the seal of the living God, calling out to the four angels to "wait" until the seal of God was placed on the foreheads of his servants. Many were sealed, 144,000 to be exact.

Then John had a second vision. The vision left earth and returned to Heaven. John saw a "vast crowd, too great to count, from every nation and tribe and people and language, standing in front of the throne and before the Lamb." Heaven is both multicultural and multilingual! And, in the midst of the diversity, there's unity. The vast crowd was clothed in white (a sign of purity) and was shouting praises to God.

7:14-17

So, who's in the crowd of people praising God? They're people coming out of the great tribulation. They've washed their robes in the blood of the Lamb. Christ cleanses our sin by his blood and we come out white. Clean! What are these believers doing? They are standing in front of the throne of God and serving him day and night. In the presence of God, there will be no hunger and no thirst. There will be no more sadness, no mental illness, no physical illness, no tears and no depression. Above all, no death! God will wipe away all of our tears!

TEACHING TREMORS

I WHAT IS WORSHIP?

Ahead of time, photocopy the student sheet on page 17 of this book. Divide your students into three equal groups. If you have more than 20 students, consider having students get in six or more groups. Give each group a copy of the reproducible sheet and a writing utensil. Give Group 2 a dictionary.

Explain, **"Our government has asked you to help with some experiments on a deserted island, but the natives on that island have other things in mind. I'd like you to work as a group to help the natives understand what worship is."**

Assign each group to work on either the "Group 1," "Group 2" or "Group 3" section of the handout. When they're finished, have groups get together with another group and explain how they answered the questions. When all groups are finished explaining, have them switch again and share their responses with a second group. When all groups have shared twice, have students gather in the center of the meeting room and talk about their own responses and the responses that they

Materials needed:
Bibles; reproducible student sheet on page 17 of this book; writing utensils; dictionary

heard from other groups. Then, lead students in a discussion by asking:

• **How easy is it to worship things other than God? Explain.**

• **Define "worship" in your own words. Based on your definitions of worship, write down some of the things *you* worship.**

• **What causes us to worship something?**

Materials needed:
Bibles; reproducible student sheet on page 18 of this book; writing utensils

II THE WORSHIP CAUSE

Have students get in five equal groups (a group can be one person). Assign each group one of the following passages: Revelation 5:1-14; Revelation 6:1-4; Revelation 6:5-8; Revelation 6:9-17; and Revelation 7:1-17. Instruct groups to read the passage, and get an idea in their minds about how they would describe it to another person.

When groups are finished, distribute copies of "The Seal Story" student sheet on page 18 of this book. Instruct groups to go to another group and have them describe the passage they read. As they are describing it, each group member must write down what they hear in the correct space provided. When each group has completed their handout, instruct groups to piece the story together from what they heard from other groups. When all groups have completed the activity, have each group read the story they wrote.

Then discuss these questions:

• **What are some of the main points you get from these passages in Revelation?**

• **Why do you think God uses this kind of symbolism?**

WHAT'S UP WITH THAT?

WHAT IS THE GREAT TRIBULATION?

The phrase "great tribulation" is only mentioned once in the Bible, here in Revelation 7:14. There are a number of different views among well-meaning Christians. One perspective is that the "great tribulation" refers to a specific time. Those who hold to this approach believe that the tribulation is a seven-year span at the end of time. The tribulation begins with the rise of the beast in Revelation 13, (the beast is also referred by some as the "Antichrist") who signs a covenant with Israel (Daniel 9:27) and the seven-year period terminates at the second coming of Jesus. This view of the tribulation is a time of God's intense wrath, judgment and destruction poured out on the earth (see Revelation 6:17; 14:7; 15:7, 8). There is debate over whether or not the Christians on earth are "taken up" (commonly referred to as "the rapture"), or are left on the earth during this horrific time of darkness, the "great tribulation," and remain until the second coming of Christ.

A second opinion concerning the great tribulation refers to the inevitable trials that have been inflicted on the church for centuries. Those who hold this viewpoint believe that God's servants will always experience persecution. Christians have suffered and died for their faith since the first century. Whether we are talking about China, Sudan, Vietnam, North Korea, Iran, Saudi Arabia or Afghanistan, people who name Christ as Lord have been beaten, raped, killed, kidnapped, flogged and tortured.

"Tribulation" has been an ongoing problem since Christ died. Many of his followers were crucified. Christians today in various places have no access to a Bible or church—primarily because it is a crime for them to be a Christian. John 16:33 promises the church will always experience tribulation. This position believes "tribulation" does not refer to a seven-year end-of-the-world period, but an ongoing struggle between good and evil, God and Satan, humans and sin.

CONTROVERSIAL Q AND A

WHO ARE THE 144,000 IN REVELATION 7?

One of the most common viewpoints is that the number 144,000 is not literal, but symbolic of God's people. The number twelve, referring to the twelve tribes of Israel, is the number of completeness. (By the way, these tribes were not even in existence at the time of John's writing!) This number mentioned by John could be suggesting that the church (God's people), is the "spiritual Israel."

One of the prominent notions states that the 144,000 are Jewish "evangelists" who have become followers of Yeshua (Jesus) during the time of the great seven-year period, the tribulation. These Jewish-Christians will be "salt and light" on the earth during that time and lead scores of people to know Christ the Messiah. Revelation 14:3 says they had been redeemed. Revelation 7:3, 4 states that God has sealed the 144,000. Whether the number is literal, or symbolic of a large number of Jewish believers, they stand triumphantly on Mount Zion (14:1-5). These messianic Jews share their faith with great boldness. They are protected and are spiritually undefiled.

COSMIC CLOSURES

JACKSON GETS REFOCUSED

Ask students to find a place in the room where they can be alone and listen. Explain to them that you're going to read a story about someone whose relationship with God got interrupted. Ask them to listen closely, because you're going to ask them to discuss it at the end.

Read the following scenario to your students:

"Jackson has been attending the same church since he was two years old. When he was ten years old, he became a Christian during a Sunday morning worship service at the same church. Since that time, Jackson has been viewed as the 'spiritual leader' of the youth group. Now he is a junior in high school. He had a steady relationship with God, that is, until he met Heather.

"In his junior year, the love bug bit Jackson. He saw Heather and immediately fell in love. Soon after they started dating they were with each other constantly—before, during and after school. At night, Jackson and Heather found ways to communicate: on the Internet, the phone or through quick visits at the mall. That was all cool until Jackson's relationship with Heather got in the way of his relationship with God.

"In the past, Jackson regularly 'met' with God nightly from 7:30-8:00 to pray and read the Bible. These days, that schedule has been trashed. Now Heather has taken over the 7:30 spot. Jackson has also stopped attending the Wednesday night Bible study so he can 'help Heather study' for Spanish, even though he doesn't know Spanish!"

After you've read the story to students, have them get in groups of two and discuss some questions. You might want to write these questions on a white markerboard or a piece of poster board so groups can discuss them at their own pace. The questions are as follows:

• **What happened to Jackson's relationship with God?**

• **How did his relationship with Heather get in the way of his relationship with God?**

Media Moment

To illustrate the kind of integrity and character that God rewards in the book of Revelation, show a clip from the movie *Remember the Titans*. Begin with the scene at 1:16:34 in which assistant coach Yost is being told, "Heck of a season the Titans are having, Coach. Too bad it's got to end." If Coach Yost throws the regional championship game, he can make the Hall of Fame. He chooses integrity over fame, and confronts one of the referees about making poor calls. The Titans end up winning the game but Yost loses the Hall of Fame. Stop the clip at 1:21:37 with the words, "Coach, I took a straw poll. You just lost yourself the Hall of Fame." This movie also illustrates well God's desire for unity among diverse cultures.

Materials needed:
Markerboard or poster board; marker

- **What happens to a relationship when one of the people gets preoccupied with another person?**
- **What advice would you give Jackson?**
- **If worship were defined by "time" (where you invest most of your time) and your "thought life" (what you think about the most), then what would you say you are currently worshiping?**

Materials needed:
Bible; CD player; worship CD; pens; paper; envelopes; postage stamps; a candle; matches

SEAL THE PLEDGE

Begin this activity by explaining, **"Many of us have let things interrupt our relationship with God. We started out in an awesome way, but over time, some thing or someone else has interfered with our intimacy with the Father. Listen to a passage from Revelation that might cause you to rethink the way you've been worshiping."**

Read Revelation 7:13-17 aloud.

Continue by saying, **"The world offers us so many things we can worship. However, Jesus is the only true, lasting focus of our worship. The more we worship him, the more he wipes our tears, and the more he feeds us. It's easy to get sidetracked and lose our focus on Christ. I'd like you to consider what has gotten in the way of your intimate relationship with God."**

Play the worship CD, and ask students to think about their relationship with God. Encourage students to use this time to search through any issue they might have. When you've given them enough time, distribute paper and pens to everyone. Explain that you'd like them to write a letter to God based on what they studied today, and encourage them to confess any distraction in their relationship to God. Students might need some coaching from you on what exactly to write. You could say, **"Perhaps you are willing to commit more time reading the Bible or praying, and cutting out something—like TV or the Internet. Consider starting with 15 minutes a day so you can learn how to love and worship Jesus."**

When students are done writing, have them seal their letters in an envelope. Ask them to self-address their envelopes. Tell students you will mail their letters to them in about two weeks, so they will need to remember the pledge they made. If you want to really make a closing impression, get a candle and seal the envelopes by melting wax on the backs of them. When Revelation was written, official documents were sealed to prevent unlawful opening and to mark their importance. Your students will be the only ones who can "break the seal."

Place the letters in the center of the meeting room, and have students gather around the letters in a prayer circle. Lead students in a short prayer, thanking God for the opportunity to worship him, and asking him to accept their letters of confession.

Be sure to remember to mail students' letters to them in two weeks. Consider giving them to an assistant to mail.

PROJECT 9
Almost Deserted Island

Our government has dropped your group onto an almost deserted island. The only inhabitants of the island are a group of about 100 natives who eat only fish and wear only clothes that wash up on the beach from passing cruise ships. Upon examining the island with one of the natives, you notice a shrine to a fish god, whom they worship in hopes of catching more fish to eat. You've got to attempt to answer your guide by following one of three scenarios.

GROUP 1

The guide for your group wants you to stop for a short time and worship the fish god. Obviously, you oppose this opportunity. The guide asks, "What is so wrong with worshiping the fish god?" Choosing not to use your Bible, your group attempts to respond to him in the following ways:

- Describe what worship is, using only your own thinking.
- Describe what the proper object of worship is.
- Explain why worshiping other things (like statues) is wrong.
- Explain what worshiping Jesus is really like.

GROUP 2

The guide for your group wants you to stop for a short time and worship the fish god. Obviously, you oppose this opportunity. The guide asks, "What is so wrong with worshiping the fish god?" One of you has a dictionary. You decide to begin using that, and hope the conversation goes well.

- Describe what worship is, using your thinking, and Webster's dictionary.
- Does Webster's dictionary give you any solid ideas about what the proper object of worship might be?
- Explain why worshiping other things (like statues) is wrong.
- Explain what worshiping Jesus is really like. (Use the dictionary if you need to.)

GROUP 3

The guide for your group wants you to stop for a short time and worship the fish god. Obviously, you oppose this opportunity. The guide asks, "What is so wrong with worshiping the fish god?" Fortunately, one of you brought a Bible. You decide to answer the native using the Bible.

- Use your Bible to describe what worship is. (Hint: Try using Psalm 95:1-7; 149:1-6; Revelation 5:11-14; 7:9-12.)
- What ideas does Scripture give you about what the object of worship might be?
- Explain why worshiping other things (like statues) is wrong.
- Explain what worshiping Jesus is really like. (Use the Bible if you need to.)

Read Revelation 5:1-14. What's happening?

Read Revelation 6:1-4. What's happening?

Read Revelation 6:5-8. What's happening?

Read Revelation 6:9-17. What's happening?

Read Revelation 7:1-17. What's happening?

THE WHOLE SEAL STORY

Below, write the entire story based on what you heard from other groups, and wrote in the spaces above.

NOT GETTING WHAT YOU DESERVE

God responds to the evil of "fallen Babylon" by unleashing judgment on earth. Seven trumpets are sounded, each signaling its own particular means of destruction. The first five trumpets were just the beginning of the massive annihilation. The sixth and seventh trumpets signified that sin has a price tag, but faith in Jesus produces victory.

OPENING SHAKES

I JUSTICE FOR ALL

Before class, acquire a local newspaper article on some current court case that has not been resolved. You will need to make four photocopies of the article.

When students have arrived, have them get into four equal groups. Give each group the same court case, and ask them to read it. After they have read the case, have groups discuss these questions:

• **What do you think the verdict will be? What do you think the verdict should be? What would be a fair and just outcome?**

• **If you were on the jury for this case, what decision would you want to make?**

• **What are some important elements in a trial?** (You will get answers like: *evidence, lawyers, jury.*) Keep pressing them until someone says "the judge."

Then ask, **"Why is the judge important?"** (*The judge determines the outcome of the person's sentence.*)

Conclude this activity by saying, **"The book of Revelation deals with justice. Revelation says that all human beings will one day stand before a judge. This judge will determine the outcome of every person's destiny. Revelation does not give all the answers to many complex questions of eternity, but we can be sure of one certainty: Jesus is that judge, and he will be fair and just. Let's see what kind of justice is in store for the end of the world."**

II THE CONSTRUCTION WORKER

Before the meeting, photocopy the skit below and recruit a student to present this monologue. It illustrates what the phrase "the wages of sin is death" really means. If you can't find a student to do this, you can either play the role yourself or get another adult who can learn the role by heart.

"I can't complain. I'm doin' all right at work, me and the wife are doin' well. What's that? *(sound of something dropping)* What do I do for a livin'? Aww, I thought you would know just by lookin' at me. I do construction. Well, I guess to be more specific, I help put on the roof. *(sigh)* I tell you what, it is tough work too. But I don't mind it I guess. You know, gotta make a livin'

LESSON TEXT
Revelation 8:1–11:19

LESSON FOCUS
The trumpets are sounded and judgment is unleashed upon the earth.

LESSON GOALS
As a result of participating in this session, students will:
• Understand the nature of God's judgment.
• Recognize that the wages of sin is death.
• Learn that the new Jerusalem is for those who fear God.

Materials needed:
Photocopies of a newspaper article

Materials needed:
A costume that includes a construction outfit, hard hat, tool belt and lunch box

somehow. The pay isn't the best, but it's not bad. I make enough to get by. And I'm proud of that too. I think a man should earn everything he gets. That's how I did it at least. All my life.

"Well, yeah, I guess I've made a couple mistakes here and there. But who hasn't? I got fired from a job one time. Five years ago. I don't think it was right though. Boss said I wasn't earnin' my keep. But anyway, that's probably all you want to hear about that. My wife? Oh, yeah, we have been together goin' on eight years now. We had her brother over for dinner on Sunday. He goes over there to the church on Krenshaw Street. He was tellin' me what the preacher said the other day. He was talkin' about how everybody sins. But I ain't killed nobody or anything like that. I follow the laws. I love my wife. I pay my bills. But he said the preacher told him that the wages of sin is death.

"So I asked him what in the world *that* means. He asked me what happens every other Friday. I said, 'Payday.' So he asked me why I get paid. I told him, 'I do my job and they pay me. I earned it.' He said that was right and that everybody that is a sinner earns something too. He said that anybody who sins earns death. I mean, he said that when you sin, even one time, you have to die. Got me thinkin'. Do I really wanna get everything that I earn?" (*walks off*)

When the monologue is over, thank your actor, then debrief with students by asking some of these questions:
• **Does everyone receive the same payment for sin?**
• **What happens to those who sin, but accepted Jesus?**
• **Do you *have* to ask forgiveness for all of your sins? Or is it okay to let the little ones go?**
Conclude, "The guy in this skit seems a little confused about what the Bible says about sin and forgiveness. Today, we'll learn about who judges sin, and why God's forgiveness is so important."

AFTERSHOCKS

If you've had to put this skit together at the last minute, consider grabbing a student from the crowd, and have him dramatically read from cue cards that you've created before the meeting.

BOOK QUAKES

REVELATION 8:1-13

When the Lamb broke the seventh seal, the praise and worship ceased for about a half hour. During this time, seven angels were handed seven trumpets. One angel appeared at the altar with a gold incense burner. It was suspended on a rope, and was used to transport fiery coals to the altar of incense. The smoke of the incense, mixed with the prayers of God's people, ascended up to God from the altar. The silence in Heaven is because the prayers of God's people were being heard. This speaks volumes about the importance of our prayer lives!

After a terrible earthquake, the first of the seven trumpets began to sound. The first trumpet produced a mix of hail, fire and blood, which were hurled to the earth. The target was vegetation. The grass, and one-third of the earth and the trees were burned up due to the lava flow.

The second trumpet brought forth a great mountain of fire (sounds like a meteor or asteroid), which was thrown into the sea, causing one-third of the waters to turn into blood. Water covers almost three-fourths of the earth's surface, so this is massive infiltration. The judgment also included freshwater contamination. Many people died because of the bitter water brought on by the third trumpet.

The fourth trumpet's judgment consisted of a breakdown of the sun, the moon and the stars. Talk about global cooling! A single eagle announced even greater terror would be forthcoming.

9:1-21

At the sounding of the fifth trumpet, a star fell to the earth. The "star" was given the "key to the shaft of the bottomless pit." Smoke poured out as though from a huge furnace. Battle-ready locusts emerged from the pit and had the power to sting like scorpions. The locusts went after those who "did not have the seal of God on their foreheads."

Those with the "seal of God" have power over sin because they have come to know the Sin-Remover! And the king of the bottomless pit is in the Greek, *Apollyon*—the Destroyer." In John 10:10, Jesus pointed out Satan's mission to destroy people. His "angels" (called demons) are described as "horses armed for battle." The war was on!

At the blasting of the sixth trumpet, four angels who had been bound were turned loose to kill one-third of the people on the earth. They led an army of 200 million troops, riding on sulfur-breathing horses. In spite of this horrendous outpouring of judgment, the people still "refused to turn from their evil deeds." God was—and still is—seeking repentance. No matter what indictment was given to the people, there was no crying for mercy, no turning toward God.

10:1-11

Revelation 10:1–11:14 is an interlude between the sixth and seventh trumpets. An angel came down from Heaven. Surrounded by a cloud and a rainbow over his head, the angel's face "shone like the sun, and his feet were like pillars of fire." Some scholars believe this is the risen Jesus; others think it is one of the chief angels. With one foot on land and one on the sea, the angel unrolled a small scroll. As the angel gave "a great shout," like the roar of a lion, the "seven thunders answered," but John was prevented from writing down what he witnessed.

The idea of the angel standing on both land and sea denotes supreme power and authority. A voice from Heaven told John to take the unrolled scroll from the angel, then the angel told him to eat it. John ate the scroll and it "was sweet in my mouth, but it made my stomach sour." The scroll represents the truth of God. Like the prophet Ezekiel who was to eat God's Word (Ezekiel 3:1-3), John was to chew on God's Word. Sometimes people can hear good news, but their stomach receives the news differently. John got a taste of what it is like to be a messenger, but it became sour when he realized that terrible judgments were about to shake the planet!

11:1-19

John measured the Temple of God, the altar and the number of worshipers. God was raising up two "witnesses" who would prophesy for a period of 1,260 days, or 3 1/2 years. The two witnesses would have the power to stop rain from Heaven, turn rivers into blood and send as many plagues upon the earth as they wished. If someone tried to harm them, they would die. But after they completed their testimony, the beast arose out of the bottomless pit and killed the two prophets. Their bodies lay in the streets of Jerusalem for three and a half days, because no one was allowed to bury them.

After three and a half days, the two witnesses resurrected and were taken up to Heaven, and terror struck everyone. In that same hour, a terrible earthquake destroyed a tenth of the city of Jerusalem and claimed 7000 lives. Everyone who did not die was terrified and gave glory to God.

The seventh trumpet was blown, and a multitude of praise erupted, proclaiming victory for Jesus and his people. The Temple of God was opened and the Ark of the covenant could be seen inside the Temple. A mighty earthquake—accompanied by lightning, thunder and a huge hailstorm, shook the world.

WHAT'S UP WITH THAT?

REVELATION IS SO HARD TO UNDERSTAND. WHAT DOES IT ALL MEAN?

There are a number of viewpoints on interpreting Revelation. "Hermeneutics" is the science and study of interpreting the Bible. If not careful, people will make Revelation say what they want it to say! The goal of hermeneutics is to rightly interpret what the author (John) originally meant when he wrote it.

Some of the images in Revelation directly correspond with Old Testament books such as Daniel and Ezekiel. The four horsemen, the seven seals, the seven trumpets, a dragon, the beast and the mark of 666 are some of the images of Revelation. Here are some common approaches to interpreting these:

The first approach to Revelation is called the *preterist* view. This interpretation states that Revelation consists of first-century events. Revelation was primarily written to encourage the Christians at a time of persecution, to offer them hope.

The *idealist* view looks at Revelation as a spiritual guidebook for the battle of good and evil. Each story is a spiritual analogy in the overall biblical landscape.

The *historicist* view takes the stance that Revelation provides a panoramic view of church history from beginning to end. There are multiple opinions within this perspective, but primarily it is seen as an historical road map.

The *futurist* sees Revelation as a book of prophecy. Revelation 4-22 is viewed as a series of literal events and people yet to take place.

The book of Revelation is the only apocalyptic literature in the New Testament. Whether you hold to a preterist, idealist, historicist or futurist viewpoint, we should all approach this book humbly and seriously.

TEACHING TREMORS

I WHAT IT REALLY MEANS

Before students enter your meeting room, you will need to write the following phrases on a markerboard or poster board:

Materials needed:
Bibles; markerboard or poster board; marker; blank paper; writing utensils

Say cheese	Put on your thinking cap
Break a leg	Scared to death
Sharp as a tack	She is the "apple of my eye"
You're my "sweetheart"	Raining cats and dogs
"Fast" food	He's in a "zone"
Get a grip	Take a hike

Begin this activity by saying, "I have written down some phrases which have images and word pictures that are *not* to be taken literally. Can you identify what each phrase really means?" *(For example, "say cheese" is a reference to smile while your picture is being taken.)*

Go through the phrases one by one, asking students to respond. Ask for a volunteer to record the responses as they are shared.

After students have completed this activity, continue by saying, **"The book of Revelation is filled with images—some are meant to be taken literally, and some are best taken figuratively. When Jesus said that he is 'the door,' he did not mean that he is a literal door with hinges. He meant that he is the pathway to the Father."**

Break into small groups of three or four and make sure that each group has a Bible, a piece of blank paper and a writing utensil. It is impossible to cover all four chapters of today's text, but this activity will allow students to skim the material. Ask groups to look at Revelation 8:1–11:19 and determine which images should be taken literally and which ones should be interpreted figuratively. (Some you might want to consider include earthquakes, trumpets, an eagle, battle-ready locusts, 200 million troops, sulfur-breathing horses, a scroll that was eaten, two prophets who are resurrected, and 1,260 days.) Your goal is not for all students to agree on their assessment of these images, but to heighten their interest in further study. Refer to the **Book Quakes** section to help answer any questions that arise. You may also want to check out the **What's Up With That?** sidebar.

II. THE SEVEN TRUMPETS

Ahead of time, photocopy the student sheet on page 25 of this book. Allow students to work through this activity in pairs. Make sure each pair has a Bible, a student sheet and a writing utensil. Give students sufficient time to look up the verses concerning the seven trumpets and then record the situations and outcomes. The first one is filled in for them as an example.

After students have completed this activity, refer to the **Book Quakes** section to deal with any questions that arise.

Comment, **"The blasting of the first six trumpets will bring about mass destruction unlike anything we have ever seen, but, for the believer in Jesus, the seventh trumpet heralds good news—the whole world is now the kingdom of our Lord and Christ."**

AFTERSHOCKS

One way to allow groups to move through the text more quickly would be to assign them smaller chunks of Scripture. Break it down into these segments: Revelation 8:1-13; 9:1-21; 10:1-11; 11:1-19. Then, allow a spokesperson from each group to share their findings.

Materials needed:
Bibles; reproducible student sheet on page 25 of this book; writing utensils

AFTERSHOCKS

If you know someone who plays trumpet, a fun way to signify that time is up for students' research would be for your trumpeter to show up outside your meeting room unnoticed by your students while they complete their work. Then, on a signal from you, he or she should blow the trumpet as loudly as possible, hopefully causing a few students to jump out of their seats.

CONTROVERSIAL Q AND A

HOW SHOULD WE INTERPRET THE SYMBOLISM IN REVELATION?

Revelation 9:7 says, "The locusts looked *like* horses armed for battle." Just like many teenagers today, John uses the word "like" often. Some take it literally and assume these are end-time demons. Take a look at their bizarre description in 9:7-10. A locust wearing a gold crown with a human face, hair like that of a woman, teeth like a lion's, a tail like a scorpion's, wearing armor made of iron?

In order to understand hermeneutics, we must know what kind of literature we are reading. When a basketball player says of the other team, "We are gonna kill them," he means, "we are going to win," not "we are going to cut their throats." It is a genre, a certain type of communication. The majority of imagery in Revelation is referred to as apocalyptic literature. The symbols, numbers, events, monsters and cataclysmic battles suggested to the people of John's day that a spiritual war existed. John wrote in a language and style that people in his day would comprehend.

One of the primary problems in the way we read Revelation is this: *We interject our times into their times, our views into their views and can misconstrue the original intent*. Perhaps a better question than asking, "Does 666 relate to a new form of identification at the grocery store?" would be "What did John mean by these symbols to the churches of Revelation?" We have spent too much time trying to decode Revelation from the perspective of the world in which we live and not enough time digging into the original intent.

Materials needed:
Videotape; TV and VCR; Bible

Materials needed:
Reproducible student sheet on page 26 of this book

COSMIC CLOSURES

I SAVED BY HIS BLOOD

Play a clip from the video *Prince of Egypt*, starting at 1:02:39 (Moses is standing on the shore, and God tells Moses to take the staff; the water turns to blood) and ending at 1:06:51 (the Egyptians run off with boils). After watching the ten plagues, discuss these questions:

• **What do you think was going through the minds of the common people then?**
• **What do you think they were feeling?**
• **How would you have felt if you had been there?**
Read Revelation 8 aloud. Then ask students:
• **What if you were there in Revelation 8?**
• **What kinds of things would be going through your mind?**
• **What would it be like to go through this experience?**

Close with saying, **"Jesus will judge every one of us. Revelation is warning us that the wages of sin is death. That is scary, but the good news is that the gift of God is eternal life through Jesus Christ. Because of what Jesus accomplished for you on the cross, you can receive Christ as Lord of your life and escape God's wrath."**

Mention to your students that you and other adult leaders are available to speak with anyone who has not yet accepted God's gift of eternal life. Be sure to tell them that this door is always open and that God's desire is for all of them to be saved, and not perish in the trumpet judgments.

II COURTROOM DRAMA: LAW AND TORTURE

Ahead of time, make six photocopies of the student sheet on page 26 of this book, and recruit six actors. Try to get them the scripts before your session begins, so that they can be familiar with their parts. Call the actors to the front and set up the sketch by saying something like this: **"The drama you are about to see takes place in a courtroom somewhere in the afterlife. This is the trial of a 'normal' teenager, whose eternal fate is about to be decided by the most Holy of Judges."**

After the sketch, close in prayer, thanking God for the blood sacrifice of Jesus that means we can be spared from judgment and have the opportunity to live with him forever in his kingdom. Second Peter 3:9 proclaims, "The Lord isn't really being slow about his promise to return, as some people think. No, he is being patient for your sake. He does not want anyone to perish, so he is giving more time for everyone to repent." Make sure your students know that you and other adult leaders are available to speak with them about this at any time.

THE SEVEN TRUMPETS

Look up the Scripture references below that are related to the seven trumpets being blown by seven angels. Then record what happens in each situation and write down the outcome. The first one is filled in for you as an example.

TRUMPETS	SCRIPTURE	SITUATION	OUTCOME
First trumpet	Rev. 8:7	Bloody hail and fire	1/3 of the trees burned up, grass burned
Second trumpet	Rev. 8:8, 9		
Third trumpet	Rev. 8:10, 11		
Fourth trumpet	Rev. 8:12		
Fifth trumpet	Rev. 9:1-12		
Sixth trumpet	Rev. 9:13-21		
Seventh trumpet	Rev. 11:15-19		

Courtroom Drama: LAW & TORTURE

Characters:
Bailiff
God (Judge)
Defendant (teenager)
Accuser (Satan)
Witness #1
Jesus (surprise witness)

Bailiff: All rise for the Honorable, Glorious, and Holy Judge!

God: Please be seated. Hello, child. Do you know why you are here?

Defendant: Yes. I mean, yes sir. Well, I mean, I think I do. My pastor told me that one day all people would be held accountable and answer for the sins they have committed. Is this that day?

God: Yes, child. The time has come for me to decide why I should let you into my kingdom.

Accuser: Or, why he should throw you out!

God: Silence!!! You will have your time, accuser. We are here in this courtroom to hear the arguments for and against, and to decide whether or not I should allow the defendant to enjoy the citizenship in my eternal kingdom. (*Bangs gavel*) Let us begin!

Accuser: Let us start with something simple, shall we? Tell us about yourself. We already know who you are, so be quick!

Defendant: Well, I'm 18 years old. I live with my mom, dad and kid brother. I play football at my high school. I also work at the grocery store right down the street from my school. I bag the groceries.

Accuser: And do you know how you came to be here today?

Defendant: I remember that I was on my way to pick up my little brother from school. I was about five minutes away from school when a dog ran into the middle of the road. I swerved to miss it, but when I did, I went into the other lane and . . .

Accuser: (*interrupts*) Well, it really doesn't matter how you came to be here. I intend to prove to the Judge that the life that you have lived has earned you an eternity apart from God. You deserve death! I call my first witness!

Bailiff: The court calls your best friend to the stand!

Accuser: Please tell the court where you were on the night of October 27.

Witness #1: I was at my house, throwing a party to celebrate our football team winning the regional playoff game.

Accuser: And were your parents there?

Witness #1: No, they were out of town on business.

Accuser: What kind of activities were people engaging in at your party?

Witness #1: We had music, dancing, a video of the big game . . .

Accuser: Go on . . .

Witness #1: Pot, and enough beer to swim in!

Accuser: Could you please tell the court where the defendant was on the night in question?

Witness #1: Well, yeah. He's the quarterback for the team! Of course he was at the party!

Accuser: . . . with his parents' knowledge and permission of course?

Witness #1: Are you nuts? They would never let him! He told them that he was staying at our wide receiver's house so they wouldn't suspect anything.

Accuser: So he lied to them and then attended a party that he knew they would never approve of?

Witness #1: Well, yeah. How else was he supposed to get there? It's just a party, right?

Accuser: No further questions. You may step down. Judge, Your law clearly states that no person who has sinned may enter into your eternal kingdom. As demonstrated by this testimony, we have heard that this boy has clearly sinned. And, I have a list of witnesses a mile long who can attest to other sins which he has committed. Clearly he does not deserve eternity in your kingdom! And, nothing that he can say or do can offer up sufficient defense for this!

God: You are correct, accuser. Nothing he can do in his own power would be a sufficient defense. But, we have not heard all the arguments yet. Bailiff, our next witness, please.

Bailiff: The court calls the surprise witness to the stand.

Accuser: So, you are going to save this child from an eternity outside of the kingdom?

Jesus: I am! Father, this child belongs to me. All the things that the accuser said are true. This child did commit all of those sins. But, he gave his life to me and asked my forgiveness for his crimes. My death has answered the payment that you demanded which he could never have hoped to pay.

God: I have heard all that I need to hear. Child, because of my Son, Jesus' testimony to your pardon, you may now rise and enter paradise. My kingdom, in all its glory, is yours. Case dismissed!

WHEN EVIL FIGHTS AGAINST YOU

The Scripture study today describes the cosmic battle between good and evil. Satan (also called the dragon) gives power to the beast and the false prophet. The dragon wants to kill the woman who's carrying a child. But Satan's plan is thwarted and the Lamb is victorious. In Chapter 13, the battle intensifies. The beast and false prophet take on the systems of this world and seduce the people of God. Those faithful to the Lamb will experience tribulation and even death, but in the end will gain eternal life.

OPENING SHAKES

I BIRTHING CLASS

Before teaching this session, obtain a short portrayal of a birth from a movie or television show. Some examples might be the clip that runs from 17:60 to 18:00 in the movie *Look Who's Talking,* or a clip from the TV show "A Baby Story."

Before students arrive, gather together as many birthing skit props as you can find. Some ideas include wet towels, sheets, extra lighting and toy babies. When students have arrived, ask them to divide into groups of four. Explain to groups that you'd like them to role-play the way they think a baby is born, keeping their presentation in good taste. Allow groups to choose whatever roles they desire (doctors, mothers, fathers, nurses, etc). When they're ready, have each group go to the front of the room and present their idea of a birth. After all groups have presented, say something like this: **"Having a child is a wonderfully scary moment. Ever wondered what it's *really* like to have a child? Let's take a look at a real birth."**

Show the clip to students. When it is over, ask, **"Did you notice the *pain* that the woman was going through in this birth? The book of Revelation also records a painful birth. The woman we are going to read about in Revelation 12 is pregnant, and today we pick up our study with her about to give birth to a son."**

II PAPER AND PEN GAME

Begin the session by saying something like, **"None of us are perfect! I'd like you to think of a time when you did something silly or stupid, and you got caught."** Give students time to remember their big mistakes. As they are thinking, ask them to write down their experiences in story form, and be sure to ask students not to put their names on their stories. When students are finished, ask them to hand you their stories. Tell students that you're going to read their stories aloud, and they must guess which story belongs to which student.

After you've read the stories and students have guessed the identity

---

LESSON TEXT
Revelation 12:1–14:13

LESSON FOCUS
The battle between good (Christ) and evil (the dragon called Satan) is explained; those who commit their lives to the Lamb will win in the end.

LESSON GOALS
As a result of participating in this session, students will:
- Learn of the battle between the woman, the child and the dragon.
- Uncover the strategies of Satan.
- Understand what it takes to win.

Materials needed:
A videotape; TV and VCR; props for impromptu birthing skits

Materials needed:
Pens and paper

of them all, say, **"Sometimes we do some pretty stupid things. God always forgives us, even when we make some pretty big mistakes. Now that you've talked about the silly things you've done, let's think about a real big thing we've done to mess up our relationship with God."**

Distribute another piece of paper to each student. Instruct students to write down the worst sin they've ever committed. Reassure them that no one (including you) is going to see this paper. If they are still intimidated tell them they can draw a symbol (such as an "X") to stand for what they are thinking about. After they have written on the paper, have them fold the paper in half, then in half again and put it in their pockets, or another safe place. Tell students to hold onto the paper until the end of the session.

BOOK QUAKES

REVELATION 12:1-18

This text describes war, but not just any kind of war. This is spiritual warfare. John saw "an event of great significance," a woman clothed with the sun, with the moon beneath her feet and twelve stars on her head. The woman was pregnant. Suddenly, there appeared a red dragon with seven heads, ten horns and seven crowns on his head. The dragon threw one-third of the stars to earth, and stood ready to devour a baby who was being birthed by the woman. The baby boy was born "to rule all nations with an iron rod" (See Psalm 2:9).

The archangel Michael and his angels fought against the dragon and his angels. The dragon lost the battle, and was kicked out of Heaven.

This dragon isn't new to believers. It's Satan! The downfall of Satan is confirmed in the Old Testament (Isaiah 14:12-17; Ezekiel 28:12-19). Notice the six descriptions of the enemy of the woman and the child mentioned in Revelation 12:1-9: "large red dragon" (v. 3); "dragon" (vv. 5, 7, 8); "great dragon" (v. 9); "the ancient serpent" (v. 9); "the Devil" (v. 9); and "Satan" (v. 9). Satan's mission is *deception*. Revelation 12:9 says the Devil is "the one deceiving the whole world." John's images help us fully understand who this ancient evil serpent really is. "The ancient serpent" is a reference to Satan in the Garden of Eden, when the serpent misled Adam and Eve (Genesis 3:1-7).

Where did Satan come from? He was a beautiful angel named Lucifer (which means "shining star" or "morning star" in Isaiah 14:12) who tried to usurp God's authority. With his attempt to be on par with God, Lucifer led a massive rebellion in Heaven and a third of the angels were excommunicated from Heaven with him. Lucifer is referred to in Revelation 12 as a deceiver, an accuser of Christians and a murderer. Jesus described Satan as a "thief" who came to "steal and kill and destroy" (John 10:10). Satan tried to kill the woman and the child. Satan is defeated by the word of our testimonies and the blood of Christ (v. 11) and therefore is angry, because he knows his time is short. As Chapter 12 comes to a close, the dragon is enraged at the woman and the rest of her children who keep the commandments of God.

13:1–14:13

A beast that had seven heads, ten horns and ten crowns on its horns arose out of the sea. Written on each of the beast's heads were names that blasphemed God. This beast has great power. Biblical scholars believe that the seven heads and ten horns refer either to past emperors of Rome or to a future world system. One of the heads of the beast had been wounded but then was miraculously healed. The dragon gave the beast power and authority to rule over everyone. Obviously, two sides in this cosmic battle emerge—those who are for God, and those who side with the dragon.

Then, another beast came up out of the earth. He called all people to worship the first beast and performed miracles in Elijah-like fashion (see 1 Kings 18:24-29) by making fire flash down to earth from Heaven. He set up an image of the first beast and made the image seem to breathe and speak. All who refused to worship the image were put to death. He required every person to be given a mark with the number 666, on their right hand or forehead. Only with this number could one buy or sell.

Chapters 12 and 13 provide a bleak picture of the two beasts that control the world. They are anti-Christ. But Chapter 14 begins with a stark contrast: a 144,000-member choir standing with the Lamb on Mount Zion, with the Lamb's and the Father's name written on their foreheads! Heaven was filled with the sounds of a roaring waterfall, a mighty thunder, many harpists playing and thousands of voices singing praise to God. The writing on "foreheads" signifies ownership, for the slave in the Scriptures was branded with his owner's mark. It also brings to mind one's "thought" life. Whereas the fallen world had given their allegiance to the two beasts, the 144,000 were placing their loyalty and dependence on the Lamb.

After this, an angel appeared, preaching the Good News. Another angel declared that Babylon is fallen. A third angel delivered the message that those who worshiped the beast would have to drink the wine of God's wrath. The startling dissimilarity is that those who worship the beast will be tormented "forever and ever," but "blessed are those who die in the Lord" (vv. 11, 13).

WHAT'S UP WITH THAT?

IS REVELATION 12 A SUMMARY OF LUCIFER'S FALL?

Some scholars believe this chapter is primarily an overview of prominent biblical history. For example, Revelation 12 seems to look at the fall of Satan, then Satan trying to kill the woman (Mary) and the baby (Jesus). Others speculate that the woman speaks of the future Israel and Satan's attempt to destroy Israel, whereas others believe it relates to the future church (people of God) during "the tribulation" and Satan's desire to kill and destroy. One thing is obvious, this chapter identifies that there is a war, a battle between life and death.

After Satan and a third of his angels were cast out of Heaven, he set off to tempt, deceive and thwart God's people. The woman was led into the wilderness, where she was given care for 1,260 days. There are differing viewpoints on this three-and-a-half year period. One outlook states that this time has to do with the middle part of the tribulation where Satan gives the antichrist of Revelation control of the earth.

Another opinion says that the 1,260 days is the time frame covering Jesus' ministry on earth, including his crucifixion, resurrection, ascension and the outpouring of the Holy Spirit. One thing is for sure—Satan falls, Satan tests and tempts, Jesus wins, Satan loses. Glad we're on the winning team!

AFTERSHOCKS

To illustrate the evil of the beast in chapter 13, play a game in which you tape a paper with a name on students' backs. The students are not to see what's on their backs. Create as many names of "evil" leaders as possible—Hitler, Mussolini, Nero, bin Laden, Genghis Khan, etc. Students must go around and can only ask "yes or no" questions, such as, "Am I alive right now?" or "Did I live in the days of Christ?" Give a prize to the person who guesses his or her name the fastest.

TEACHING TREMORS

I A PICTURE OF EVIL

Begin this activity by saying, **"Today we're talking about some difficult images. So, I'd like you to work together to picture each of the three main characters in Revelation 12."**

Have students get in three equal groups. Give each group a copy of the "Good Vs. Evil" reproducible student sheet on page 34, pens and one large sheet of blank paper. Assign each of the groups to either research the Woman, the Red Dragon or the Male Child. Ask the groups to look up the Scripture verses listed below the image they've been assigned. After they've read and discussed the passages, ask them to draw a picture that represents what they learned about their assigned person.

When all groups are done, let them take turns presenting their drawings to the whole group. Then discuss these questions:
- **What parts do each of these people play in Revelation?**
- **Why do you think God uses this imagery?**
- **What is the significance of God using a woman, a dragon and a male child to accomplish his will?**

Conclude by saying, **"This activity helps us understand a little better why evil exists in the world. Because Satan knows his days are numbered, he is doing everything he can to war against the people of God. But, we have the assurance that if we will fight on the side of the Lamb, ultimate victory will be ours."**

II THE BATTLE EPOCH

Begin by saying, **"The images and people of Revelation 12-14 aren't just flat pictures; they are actually doing things. I'd like you to look more at what each of these characters is involved in."**

Tape photocopies of the "One Nasty Fight" student sheet in ten different locations throughout your meeting room. Instruct students to go to each handout alone with only their Bibles. Make sure each student has a Bible and something to write with. Instruct students to begin at whatever number they want, go to a particular sheet, read the passage and write their answer on the handout. You'll end up with a lot of answers on each handout. Encourage students to remain totally silent as they work through the answers. After students have answered all ten of the questions, ask them to get in groups of three and discuss the following questions:
- **What are the major themes in these verses?**
- **What did you learn about the spiritual world from this study?**
- **What did you learn about the beast from these passages?**
- **What do these verses tell you about Satan?**

Comment, **"We can thank God that we do not have to confront the dragon, the first or second beast by ourselves. We stand in the strength of the One who defeated him. He is worthy of all our praise! No matter what we may have to endure for his sake, he promises that if we remain faithful to the end, we will be rewarded with an eternity spent in his presence."**

Materials needed:
Bibles; reproducible student sheet on page 34 of this book; writing utensils; blank paper

Media Media Media

Moment

Show a clip from the movie *Star Wars: Return of the Jedi*. Begin at 1:50:44 and end at 1:53:40. The dialogue begins: "You cannot hide forever, Luke. Give yourself to the dark side." Luke Skywalker and Darth Vader battle. The clip closes with Luke saying, "I'll never turn to the dark side. You failed, your heiness (speaking to the emperor)." The emperor says, "So be it, jedi." The powerful implication of this scene is the reality of warfare; we are in a spiritual (invisible), yet very real conflict with the enemy.

Materials needed:
Bibles; reproducible student sheet on page 35 of this book; masking tape; writing utensils

---

CONTROVERSIAL Q AND A

WHO IS THE "BEAST" (ANTICHRIST) IN REVELATION 13?

Did you know the term "Antichrist" isn't in the book of Revelation? It is used in 1 John 2:18, 22; 4:3; and 2 John 7. This term was used to describe any person or spirit that was anti-Christ, in opposition to Jesus Christ. People have speculated over the years if a superpower "God-like" world leader would emerge—one who personifies evil (aka Satan). The referencing to this antichrist began in the Roman Empire, with Emperor Nero (who persecuted Christians) being viewed as the "beast." Many names have surfaced over the course of time, including Hitler, Mussolini and Stalin. It has gotten wacky at times, with such names being suggested as the Pope, Bill Clinton, Marilyn Manson and even Bill Gates!

There are at least two common positions concerning the "beast." The first view is a *literal* one. The authors of the *Left Behind* series align themselves with a literal antichrist who takes over the world, and gives a literal mark of *666*. This mark (perhaps invisible to the naked eye) allows some to purchase foods and goods, while those without the mark will suffer physically without food and basic material needs. This literal view states that the beast has had a miraculous recovery from a head injury and either is "resurrected" or fakes a near-death experience. This "antichrist" will rise to world power and will be worshiped. The mark of *666* is viewed as one number short of the perfect number, seven, and therefore the implication is the Antichrist wants to be God but will always come up short and be only a man.

The other perspective is much more *spiritual* in nature. This view presumes that the spirit of the "beast" is all around us daily, and all one needs to do is look. History reveals that every generation has had an antichrist spirit, and that a number of people exhibit this hatred toward Christ. Placing a mark on one's forehead speaks to "garbage in, garbage out." What one places in his or her mind determines the outcome of one's life.

The Bible warns against foolish speculation. Some read with a Bible in one hand and a newspaper in the other trying to "discern" the true identity of the antichrist. Our concern should not be, "Who is the beast?" but rather, "Who will I worship, the Lamb or the beast?" Let God take care of the details.

AFTERSHOCKS

Find out if any of your students believe that the antichrist (beast) is a "real" person and if they feel the antichrist is alive on earth today. Lead a short, lively discussion using any of the information in the **Book Quakes** or **Controversial Q and A** sections to help you out.

COSMIC CLOSURES

I MY GROUP THINKS . . .

Ahead of time, write the questions and case studies below on 3" x 5" index cards. If you're short on time, just photocopy this page and circle the questions and situations that you'd like students to discuss.

Say something like this: **"I'd like to get your opinion on some of the tougher questions that arise from these passages of Scripture."**

Have students get in small groups of three to five people, and give each group one of the cards with both the questions and situation on it. Allow groups to spend time working on their assignments. When groups are ready, let them take turns sharing the answers to the questions, and the solutions to their situations.

Then ask:

• **Why would Satan want to accuse Christians before God day and night? Be prepared to give the rest of the groups several good reasons.**

• **What are some of Satan's "favorite" areas in which he accuses believers? Explain three or four, with some of your own ideas concerning why these are his favorites.**

• **Discuss the differences between conviction and condemnation.**

Materials needed:
Bibles; 3" x 5" index cards; writing utensils

Say, **"If you're stumped about the difference between condemnation and conviction, let me read to you the difference, along with something from the book of Romans."**

Read students the following differences between condemnation and conviction, along with the Romans passage printed below.

Conviction	Condemnation
Is God-focused	Is self-focused
Leads to change	Leads to frustration
Freeing	Legalistic
Freedom from guilt	Feeling not good enough
Brings peace	Creates guilt
Provides a new start	Causes remorse
Confession brings closure	Brings a feeling of being unable to change

Then read Romans 8:1, 2 in *The Message*:

"With the arrival of Jesus, the Messiah, that fateful dilemma is resolved. Those who enter into Christ's being-here-for-us no longer have to live under a continuous, low-lying black cloud. A new power is in operation. The Spirit of life in Christ, like a strong wind, has magnificently cleared the air, freeing you from a fated lifetime of brutal tyranny at the hands of sin and death."

Comment, **"It can be extremely difficult to know if we're being convicted by God, or condemned by Satan. I'd like you to talk about the difference in the following situations."**

Have groups discuss the following case studies and decide if each incident is conviction from God or condemnation from Satan.

Case One:

Katie lied to her mom three weeks ago about where she and her friends went on Friday night. Although she confessed it to her parents, and to God, she still feels guilty.

Case Two:

Matt went to a movie with some of his friends. In the middle of the movie there was a scene that was very sexual in nature. He began to think about the challenge for purity and holiness laid out by his small group leader a few weeks earlier. He started feeling sick inside and contemplated walking out of the movie.

Ask for student response to these questions:
• **What advice would you give to Katie? To Matt?**
• **Is it always easy to know the difference between conviction and condemnation?**

Conclude by saying, **"Satan wants us to feel condemned, but God wants us to feel convicted. When we listen to Satan and allow ourselves to feel condemned, it's easier for us to sin and really mess up our relationship with God. Let's confess our sins before God, and respond to his conviction."**

SILENT CONFESSION

Begin this closing activity by saying something like this: **"God convicts us for a reason. It's the best way he can get us to respond to our sin."**

Allow students a few minutes to think about what they wrote on their papers at the beginning of the session (the worst sin they'd ever committed). As students are thinking, place the "Throne" in the center of the room.

Say, **"Look. Satan is out to get you. He succeeds in discouraging you by reminding you over and over about all of the wrong things you've done. But God is out to save you. And his goal is to convict you of your sin so you'll turn from it, not so you'll continue to sin more. Whatever sin we've committed, we've got to confess it to God, and turn it completely over to him."**

Point out the "Throne" in the center of the room. Encourage students to go to the throne, and spend a few minutes in prayer. Students might pray about the condemnation they feel, or about the conviction that God has placed on them. After they've prayed, encourage students to place their sins on the seat.

After all students have left their sins at the throne, close your time together by thanking God for forgiving them of their sins.

Materials needed:

A throne (Ideas: a wingback chair, a chair from your church's platform, a chair draped with royal-looking fabric)

Media Moment

While students are leaving their sins on the throne, play the song, "You Are My King (Amazing Love)," recorded on the CD *Passion '99: Better Is One Day*.

GOOD VS. EVIL

GROUP 1

Isaiah 26:13-18

Isaiah 54:1

Isaiah 66:6-11   WOMAN =

Micah 4:9, 10

Matthew 2:13-15

GROUP 2

Revelation 12:9

Revelation 20:2

John 8:44   RED DRAGON=

Daniel 7:7, 23-25

GROUP 3

Revelation 12:5

Psalm 2:7-12

Luke 1:26-35   MALE CHILD =

Philippians 2:5-11

one. Who are the main characters in this chapter? (Revelation 12:1-5)

two. Why would the dragon seek to devour the baby? (12:4)

three. Compare Ezekiel 28:14-19 with Revelation 12:5-9. What do you learn about the dragon?

four. What effect does the dragon's defeat have on Heaven? (12:10-12)

five. What effect does the dragon's defeat have on earth? (12:13-17)

six. What do you learn about the beast from these verses? (13:1-10)

seven. What new power is given to the beast? (13:11-18)

eight. Chapter 14 refers to angels. What are they doing?

nine. What happens to those who worship the beast? (14:9-12)

ten. What words of encouragement are given to those who worship Jesus? (14:13)

One Nasty Fight

GOD'S PLANS FOR AN UGLY STREETWALKER

Seven angels carry seven bowls that contain the seven last plagues of God's wrath. These bowls emerge with great intensity and fierceness, mightily displaying God's power in the midst of fallen Babylon. While the wicked people of the earth are being slaughtered by God's judgment, those who have been victorious over the beast (by not receiving his mark or worshiping his image) are rewarded by God. Is this the "end of the world as we know it"?

OPENING SHAKES

I CIRCLE THE WAGONS

Before the session begins, arrange chairs in a circle with one less chair than there are students. After everyone has arrived explain that you are going to play a short game that has something to do with the theme of today's study. Assign a person to be "it." To begin the game, this person should point to someone and ask, "Who are your neighbors?" Within five seconds if that person cannot say the names of two neighbors on either side of him, he is "it." If he *does* say his neighbors' names within five seconds, then the person who is "it" should ask him what he likes about one of his neighbors. If he responds, "because he is wearing blue jeans," then everyone who is wearing jeans has to get up and move chairs. The person who does not get a seat is "it" for the next round. The criteria for who has to get up and move changes each round depending on the person's response.

After your students have played a half-dozen rounds of this, conclude by saying, **"The action of this game was fast and furious. You were singled out and had to move based on what you are wearing. In our study of Revelation today we are going to examine a time in the future when God's wrath and justice will be poured out on those who did not choose to follow the Lamb. It will be a time of destruction and chaos for all who have chosen to follow the beast."**

II ORDER IN THE COURT?

Begin this activity by saying, **"We live in a society today in which people are sued every day for all kinds of silly reasons. If you were the judge how would you rule in these lawsuits?"** (Read each of the situations below, and pause for student response.)

1. **A woman sued a Las Vegas casino for $350,000 (she lost the money playing blackjack one weekend). She claimed that it was the casino's responsibility to tell her that she was a lousy card player.**
   • **How would you rule in this situation?**

- **Does everyone agree with that response?**
- **On what basis would you render your judgment?**

2. A student in Tennessee tripped on his school steps and broke his finger. His parents sued the cement manufacturing company for $75,000.
- **How would you rule in this situation?**
- **Does everyone agree with that response?**
- **On what basis would you render your judgment?**

Conclude by saying something like this: **"Judges in our land must deal with all kinds of crazy lawsuits. Their job is to render a judgment based on the way they read a particular law. At the end of the world, the ultimate Judge, God, will administer justice to the whole world. Those who have chosen to follow him will be pardoned, but those who have rebelled against him will receive punishment unlike any the world has ever known. Let's dig in to Revelation to see God's plan for the end of the world."**

BOOK QUAKES

REVELATION 14:14-20

The "Son of Man" (Jesus) appeared sitting on a white cloud, wearing a golden crown (signifying him as conqueror) and carrying a sharp sickle in his hand. This sharp tool for cutting grain suggests the decisive judgment to come. An angel came from the "Temple" (the presence of God) and announced the imminent harvest, a time to gather in the righteous and the lost. The great winepress of God's wrath represents the judgment of God, the verdict that would send the lost forever away from God's presence.

15:1-8

In John's next vision, he saw those who had been victorious over the beast now holding harps, "singing the song of Moses" (see Exodus 15 and the song of deliverance) and declaring God's greatness. God's Tabernacle in Heaven was "thrown wide open." The seven final plagues were about to be poured out. The "bowl" was a shallow vessel used for drinking. The Temple was filled with smoke from God's glory and power. No one could enter the Temple until the seven angels had completed pouring out the seven plagues. We need a renewed sense of how Isaiah felt before the presence of God—totally unworthy! (see Isaiah 6:1-7). God is holy and we are not!

16:1-21

Then John saw seven angels pour out the seven plagues of God's wrath from seven bowls. The first angel poured out a bowl of "horrible, malignant sores" (see Exodus 9:9-11) that fell on those with the mark of the beast. One by one, each bowl was poured out on the earth, administering the final terms of God's justice. The seas, rivers and springs turned to blood and the sun scorched people's skin—and yet, with all the torment, people still refused to repent of their evil deeds.

The Euphrates River dried up and there was an earthquake greater than ever before in human history. Hollywood produced the movies *Deep Impact* and *Armageddon*, but they pale in comparison to the description here of the cataclysmic destruction to come. The islands disappeared, the mountains were leveled and there were terrible hailstorms with hail weighing 75 pounds! Once again, rather than turning to God, people cursed him because of the hailstorm.

17:1-8

Babylon is a city, but at the time of John's writing, it did not exist anymore. John used Babylon symbolically to refer to Rome, just as he referred to a treacherous woman named Jezebel in Revelation 2:20 to describe something else symbolic. "Babylon" represents a world system gone astray from God's purposes. Babylon's crimes included immorality and blasphemies against God, and the persecution of his saints. This "great prostitute" will receive God's final, just and complete judgment.

17:9-18

John saw a scarlet beast that had seven heads and ten horns. The heads represented the seven hills of the city where the woman rules. (Rome was known as the city of seven hills. If the woman sitting on the beast is Rome, then the beast is The Roman Empire.) In his commentary on Revelation, William Barclay referred to the seven kings (Roman emperors), five of whom had already fallen—Augustus, Tiberius, Caligula, Claudius and Nero. (*The Daily Bible Studies, The Revelation of John*, p. 146). The sixth ruler still alive when John wrote these words was Vespasian, and the seventh is a reference to Titus. There was one more ruler, an eighth king yet to come. Some speculation is that John envisioned Nero to be replaced by this new super-leader in Domitian.

The ten kings represented by the ten horns (v. 12) probably refer to the world rulers who would overtake Rome, or would take on the future Antichrist. These rulers will attempt to overpower the Lamb but he will overcome because the Lamb is the "Lord over all lords." The prostitute (Babylon or Rome) had influenced people of every nation and language, yet ultimately she would be destroyed.

18:1-24

An angel descended from Heaven with the proclamation that "Babylon is fallen—that great city is fallen!" The city was polluted with demons and evil spirits and God's people were told to flee because of her great wickedness. God was going to judge Babylon for her idolatry, pride and greed. Babylon had succumbed to the love of money (see 1 Timothy 6:10). At the time of John's writing, Rome was known for its wealth, as evidenced by its silver dishes and precious stones. When people leave a legacy, they are passing down their values to others coming after them. Babylon passed on the legacy of greed. And those who had enjoyed the spoils of her materialism were mourning because the party was over. They were totally self-absorbed!

Not only did the merchants and the rulers bemoan Babylon's downfall, so did the sea captains and their crews. As Rome is destroyed, Heaven celebrates because God is in control and evil has been eradicated. It is imperative that we learn to look at life from God's "lens" rather than from the world system in which we live (Babylon). For John's day it was the influence of the Roman Empire. What is it for us today in the 21st-century?

WHAT'S UP WITH THAT?

WHAT IS GOD'S PLAN FOR HUMANITY?

After reading these chapters in Revelation, it might seem like God enjoys sending judgment, but quite the contrary. God the Father, Son and Holy Spirit want men and women everywhere to come to the wedding feast of the Lamb. God's desire is that none should perish! He wants all people to come to Christ (John 3:16; Revelation14:14-16). Christ has paved the way for humanity to have a relationship with God now and forever, but God will not force himself on anyone. He is patient in waiting for people to change (2 Peter 3:9). It is time for the harvest. Christ died and rose again for all to have eternal life. Yet we have seen in our study of Revelation the stark reality that many will refuse to come clean before the Lamb. Sin has a price tag. It must be punished. And faith will be rewarded.

TEACHING TREMORS

I THE END OF THE WORLD AS WE KNOW IT?

Ahead of time, photocopy the student sheet on page 43 of this book. Begin this activity by saying something like this: "**Many people speculate concerning how the world will end. Will it be with a cataclysmic earthquake, or a huge world war somewhere in the Middle East? No one knows exactly all that will take place. But one thing is for sure—it will be on God's terms. His patience for enduring the wickedness of mankind is wearing thin and there will come a day when he will pronounce judgment.**"

Ask students to get in groups of three to five. Make sure that each group has a student sheet, at least one Bible and something to write with. Allow groups sufficient time to read the Scripture and answer the questions. The bulk of the material on their handout deals with the seven bowls of God's wrath. Encourage them to just skim chapters 17 and 18. After all groups have completed their work, bring the groups back together. You'll need to help them understand the significance of "Babylon." Refer to the material in the **Book Quakes** section.

Then discuss these questions as a group:

• **Which plague poured out of the bowls of God's wrath seems the worst to you?**

• **Why is God so angry?**

• **If "Babylon" was the Roman Empire in Paul's day, what is the warning for us today?**

II WHAT'S IN A NAME?

Before the session begins, photocopy the student sheet on page 44 so that each student will have a copy. Begin this activity by saying, "**We've run across a lot of names in our study of Revelation—names like the Lamb, Apollyon, the great red dragon, the beast and the Son of Man. Let's look at our Scripture today and discover some names for God, the ultimate Judge who will bring the world to an end.**"

Distribute writing utensils and copies of the reproducible student sheet on page 44. To have some fun with this activity, before students dig into the names of God, they are to guess which names are real and

Materials needed:
Bibles; reproducible student sheet on page 43 of this book; writing utensils

Materials needed:
Reproducible student sheet on page 44 of this book; writing utensils

which might be false. *(All names are true except* Ywanda Snack; Heaven, Michigan; Belching, Tennessee; *and* Hell, Wisconsin. *The cities and states are as follows: The Motor City—*Detroit, Michigan; *The Big Apple—*New York, New York; *The Windy City—*Chicago, Illinois; *The Queen City—*Cincinnati, Ohio; *The Sunshine State—*Florida; *The Bluegrass State—*Kentucky; *The Lone Star State—*Texas.)

The names for God they should discover include: *Lord God Almighty, King of the Nations* (Revelation 15:3, 4); *Holy One, Lord God Almighty* (16:5, 7); and *Lord over all lords and King over all kings* (17:14).

Conclude by saying, **"Would you rather be on the side of the One who is King and Lord over all, or the world system that is described in Revelation 17:5 as 'Mother of All Prostitutes and Obscenities in the World'? Duh! We can thank God that he has named us to be his 'chosen and faithful ones' (17:14)."**

CONTROVERSIAL Q AND A

CAN YOU EXPLAIN ARMAGEDDON?

Armageddon is mentioned only once in the entire Bible, in Revelation 16:16. Megiddo was a town on a plain located at the base of a hill called Mount Megiddo, or Armageddon. This city overlooks the Jezreel valley. Many bloody and decisive battles in Israel's history have been fought there, and contemporary culture often speaks of the Battle of Armageddon. What is the big deal over a verse that is mentioned only once in the Bible? Many people believe that there will be a series of battles at the end of the age, and this will be the final battleground between the forces of good and evil. The War of Armageddon is, says Mark Hitchcock, "the climactic event of the great Tribulation" (*101 Answers to the Most Asked Questions About The End Times*, Multnomah, © 2001, Sisters, Oregon, p. 190). Hitchcock contends that the battle will be in Israel, with "armies of the world" gathered and will be dismantled by the Lord Jesus (p. 198).

The alternative view is that Armageddon refers to a spiritual battle in which God will declare triumph over his enemies. In other words, this is not a physical encounter.

AFTERSHOCKS

Pick up a copy of *Magnetic Teaching*, by Rick Bundschuh (Standard Publishing). It is loaded with some excellent ideas for active learning.

COSMIC CLOSURES

I VALUES WATCH

Ahead of time, you will need to record a few commercials that portray certain values in our world system today—things like good looks, corporate success, the accumulation of possessions and athletic achievement. Begin this activity by saying something like this: **"Today we've taken a look at the values of greed, idolatry and pride exemplified in Babylon, or the Roman Empire. But, what about us? What kind of values are we fed in our world today?"**

Roll the tape and ask your students to do a "values" check. After they have watched the commercials, discuss these questions:

- **Which of the ads are true?**
- **Which are deceptive?**
- **Which values stand opposed to what God desires for our lives?**
- **Can you think of other values in our world that were not portrayed in these ads?**
- **In what ways can we be deceived in our culture?**

Then say, **"Here are some subjects that communicate certain**

Materials needed:
Blank videotape; TV and VCR

Materials needed:
Bibles; markerboard or poster board; marker

values." After mentioning each of the following, ask, **"What is the value communicated?"** After each one, allow for student response.

- Name a popular TV show.
- Name a current movie.
- Choose a current style of clothing or fashion.
- Show a current teen magazine advertisement.
- Mention a "Hollywood relationship" gone sour.
- Name a particular car.
- Choose a current popular song.

Conclude by saying, **"Just as God was upset with the values he saw demonstrated in Babylon, he is also extremely concerned with some of the things he sees going on in our society. Ultimately, he is the Judge of what values will last at the end of time, and what values will be forever destroyed."**

Close in prayer, asking God to help you get on the same page with the things he values, and praising him for the opportunity to be saved from an eternity spent away from his presence.

II HERE COMES THE JUDGE

Begin by saying, **"Everyone will face the judgment of God when he or she dies. But the outcome of the judgment will not be the same for everyone."** Divide your students into two groups and have them look up Scripture verses and give brief explanations of what happens when unbelievers and believers die. For Group 1, write the following verses on the board and ask them to explain what happens to the unbeliever when he or she dies: Matthew 13:40-42; 25:41-46; Revelation 20:11-15. For Group 2, write the following verses on the board and ask them to explain what happens to the believer in Jesus when he or she dies: Matthew 25:31-36; John 3:15; 5:29; Philippians 3:20; 1 Thessalonians 4:17.

Ask for a volunteer from each group to summarize their findings. After they have done so, ask, **"Do you know what the outcome will be when you are judged at the end of your life? If you are unsure, you can leave today being sure."** You will need to be sensitive and read your students. Briefly explain the plan of salvation and then close in prayer. Tell your group that you are available if they have any questions or if they want to know for sure what will happen when they die. This is the most important decision of their lives.

In Revelation 14:14-20, what is the harvest?

What are the people singing about in chapter 15, and how does their song express God's heart for the nations?

There are seven bowl judgments in chapter 16. Look up the Scripture verses below, and then decide the situation and the outcome of each bowl. The first one is filled in for you as an example.

BOWLS	SCRIPTURE	SITUATION	OUTCOME
First	Revelation 16:2	poured over the earth	malignant sores broke out on those with the beast's mark
Second	Revelation 16:3		
Third	Revelation 16:4-7		
Fourth	Revelation 16:8, 9		
Fifth	Revelation 16:10, 11		
Sixth	Revelation 16:12-16		
Seventh	Revelation 16:17-21		

What does "Babylon" mean in chapters 17 and 18?

How is evil personified in chapters 17 and 18?

What is God's main message to his people in chapter 18?

What's in a Name?

Which names do you think are real and which ones are fake?

Anita Bath	Jim Shoe
Bill Board	April Showers
Mary Christmas	Ywanda Snack
Barb B. Cue	Bea Sting
Kitty Litter	Mitch Suebeshi
Ella Mentry	Lou Tenant
Rick O'Shay	Phylis Up
Harry Pitts	Sue Zuki
Forrest Ranger	

Now for some city trivia. Which ones are real cities and which ones are not?

Bug, Kentucky	Pee Pee, Ohio
Ordinary, Kentucky	Belching, Tennessee
Madonna, Maryland	Yell, Tennessee
Heaven, Michigan	Cut and Shoot, Texas
Goodfood, Mississippi	Jot 'Em Down, Texas
Busy, New York	Looneyville, Texas
Stiff Knee Knob, North Carolina	Virgin, Utah
	Hell, Wisconsin

Identify these titles with the cities or states that correspond to them:

The Motor City	The Sunshine State
The Big Apple	The Bluegrass State
The Windy City	The Lone Star State
The Queen City	

Read the following verses and record the different names of God.

Revelation 15:3, 4	Revelation 16:5, 7	Revelation 17:14

WELCOME TO THE RAVE!

The Scripture study today depicts Heaven's celebration of the defeat of Satan. At last has come the time for the wedding feast of the Lamb. The Son of God appears riding on a white horse, and with him are the armies of Heaven riding on white horses, and dressed in pure white linen. Purity has overcome impurity! The world system, known as Babylon, has been dethroned. The millennium, or thousand-year reign, begins, and all persons are judged in what is known as the "Great White Throne Judgment."

OPENING SHAKES

I THE BEST OF TIMES, THE WORST OF TIMES

After all your students have arrived, begin your session by saying, **"Sometimes the best of times and the worst of times happen simultaneously. For example, the end of a war is the best of times because we have reached a peaceful agreement with our enemy and ended the horrors of war. But it is also the worst of times as people mourn the loss of loved ones and begin the process of rebuilding their lives."**

Show a clip from the movie *City Slickers* where Mitch, Phil and Ed share memories from their lives and Ed's best day and worst day are the same. The clip runs from 1:13:48 to 1:15:47. After the clip, ask students to discuss this question:

• **How can someone's best day be the same as his worst day?**

Next, ask for several volunteers to share a story of the best or worst day of their lives. Be prepared to share one of your life stories to get things started or to keep it moving.

Conclude by saying, **"Today's session is one of those best of times/worst of times. It is the best of times as Jesus rides in victoriously and hurls Satan to his terminal fiery home. Yet, it will be the worst of times for those who have not trusted in Jesus—they will find themselves at the same destination as Satan."**

II THERE'S A PARTY GOING ON RIGHT HERE

Ahead of time, tape some signs to the walls in your room that say things like, "Welcome Home," "Congratulations," "I've Been Waiting" and "Well Done!" Recruit an adult or student leader to dress up as Jesus and stand outside the door of your meeting room. He should be holding a large book labeled, "The Book of Life." As students arrive, have "Jesus" ask for their names and pretend to search

---

LESSON TEXT
Revelation 19:1–20:15

LESSON FOCUS
Songs of victory fill the streets of Heaven as the Victor rides in and vanquishes the loser.

LESSON GOALS
As a result of participating in this session, students will:
• Establish why the residents of Heaven are celebrating.
• Unmask the rider on the white horse.
• Interpret the millennium, the defeat of the dragon and the final judgment.

Materials needed:
Videotape; TV and VCR

Materials needed:
Signs; masking tape; white robe; crown; Lamb's "Book of Life"; cake and ice cream; party goods; upbeat worship music; CD player

through the book and find their names, then allow them to enter. Students will enter the room to find a celebration waiting for them—complete with cake, ice cream and the works. Play some upbeat worship music in the background.

After everyone has had a chance to celebrate, begin the session by asking these questions:
- **Why do people celebrate?**
- **What is the biggest celebration you have ever witnessed?**
- **What is the biggest celebration you could imagine?**

Comment, **"Today's session is about God's biggest celebration, so what do you say? Let's get this party started!"**

BOOK QUAKES

REVELATION 19:1-16

Heaven shouts the defeat of Babylon and the exaltation of God. Just as we saw in Chapter 4, the 24 elders and the four living creatures are praising God. After the announcement for the wedding feast of the Lamb was made, the apostle John fell down to worship, but was told not to! (Angels don't want to be worshiped!)

The rider on the white horse appears, and it is Jesus—the one who is Faithful and True! (Some refer to verse 11 as "the second coming of Christ.") The book of Revelation makes it very clear that Jesus is the judge, and when all stand before God's throne, Jesus is the arbitrator! His judgment will be fair and objective, unlike our judgments—which are usually subjective. Jesus is described with eyes as bright as flames of fire, wearing many crowns on his head, clothed with a robe dipped in blood and his title was the "Word of God." John 1:14 referred to Jesus as "the Word [who] became human and lived here on earth among us." Here Jesus is known as the "King of kings and Lord of lords."

19:17–20:10

An angel announces a great war. The beast gathered the rulers of the earth to wage war against Jesus and his army of warriors and white horses, but the defeat of the beast and the false prophet was decisive. They were thrown alive into the sulfur-burning lake of fire. The sharp sword that came out of Jesus' mouth killed their entire army. And the vultures gorged themselves on the dead bodies!

Chapter 20 opens with the binding of Satan for a thousand years (the millennium). The Devil was thrown into the "bottomless pit" so that he could not deceive the nations anymore until the thousand years were up. Following the millennial kingdom, Satan is let out of his prison, where he once again gathers an army to battle the people of God. Fire from Heaven comes down and consumes the attacking armies of Satan. Satan himself is eventually thrown into the lake of fire where he, the beast and the false prophet will be tormented day and night forever and ever.

20:11-15

These verses provide the chilling conclusion to humanity, as we know it, commonly called the "Great White Throne Judgment." On that day, everyone "both great and small" will stand before God's throne. There is a mention of "the books" and the "Book of Life." The dead were judged according to what they had done. Death and the grave were thrown into the lake of fire. And anyone whose name was not found in the Book of Life was thrown into the lake of fire.

WHAT'S UP WITH THAT?

ARE WE LIVING IN THE MILLENNIUM?

These are the predominant views on this controversial subject:

1. Premillennial

This view states that Christ will literally return physically after the great tribulation (seven-year period), defeat his foes in the battle of Armageddon and rule the earth a literal thousand years. (Millennium means "one thousand.") Premillennialism contends that Christ will come before (pre-) the millennial kingdom. In fact, the second coming of Christ inaugurates the millennium. Premillennialism was the view of the early church until the third century, when amillennialism seemed to take its place.

2. Amillennial

This perspective holds that the thousand-year reign is figurative, not literal. Christ will rule, but not a literal thousand years. The Roman Catholic Church, Greek Orthodox and a number of Protestant denominations hold this view. Amillennialists believe that the rule of Christ is right now, which happens in the hearts of his believers, and the millennium will end at the second coming of Christ.

3. Postmillennial

This view is similar to amillennialism because it also does not hold to a literal thousand-year reign of Christ. Jesus' rule exists now until the second coming. Believers are to preach the gospel until the second coming. Christ will return to earth after (post-) the millennium. Therefore, the millennium (figurative) started at the first coming and ends at the second coming of Jesus Christ.

4. Panmillennial

This is a play off the others, which in essence says, "I don't know. I just believe it will all 'pan out' in the end!" Tony Campolo has remarked, concerning the second coming of Christ, "I'm not on the program committee—I'm on the welcoming committee!"

AFTERSHOCKS

Spend some time cross-referencing some of the passages in Revelation with their roots in the Old Testament. This emphasizes the continuity throughout all of God's Word. Here are just a few to consider: the beast out of the sea (Revelation 13:1-8; Daniel 7); the cup of God's wrath (Revelation 14:9-12; Jeremiah 25:15-29); the fall of Babylon (Revelation 18:1-3; Isaiah 21:1-10); and no more tears in Heaven (Revelation 21:4; Isaiah 25:1-8).

TEACHING TREMORS

I CAN I GET AN AMEN! HALLELUJAH!?

Ahead of time, make enough photocopies of the student script on page 51 so that all participants can have one. To enhance the production, make some signs for the 24 elders, the four living creatures and Jesus ("Faithful and True," "Word of God," "King of kings and Lord of lords").

Recruit some students from your group to be participants in a melodrama. Comment, **"A melodrama is a drama in which the narrator tells a story and the participants act out what he or she is saying. In this case, we are going to act out an incredible scene from the Bible. It's found in Revelation 19."** The narrator should be an adult leader or mature student who is familiar with the script. The narrator should also play the part of the director when the chorus sings. You may also want to choose your participants ahead of time and give

Materials needed:
Photocopies of the reproducible script on page 51 of this book; actors; appropriate props (signs, a robe, a Bible and a sword)

them a copy of the script. However, this can be performed with no preparation on the part of the actors. If your group is small or you need a good laugh, have two students attempt to act out all the parts themselves! The text is taken from the New Living Translation. Tell "the nations" ahead of time that when the "nations" are mentioned, they are to fall to the floor!

When everyone is in place, have your students present the melodrama. Make sure the narrator pauses for all the characters to perform the actions that are mentioned in the narration. Some of the action will be serious, and some of it will be funny. After students have acted out the drama, thank all the participants and ask them to be seated.

Close this activity by saying something like this: **"A lot of dramatic things take place in this section of Scripture. We hear Heaven singing praises and proclaiming God's eternal authority. Heaven opens up and the mystery Man rides in and conquers evil. We see the power of God and the humiliation of evil as the birds of the air eat the flesh of the world's greatest leaders. It will be one fantastic ending far beyond any special effects in any movie ever made. I want to be on the winning side, don't you?"**

II THE INS AND OUTS OF HEAVEN

Before the session begins, photocopy the student sheet on page 52. Begin this activity by asking students to respond to this question: **"When you think about Heaven, what kinds of images come to mind?"**

Allow several students to share some of their ideas concerning what Heaven will be like. Try not to comment on the validity or impossibility of any idea shared. Simply let them share some of their brainstorms. We'll talk more about Heaven in the next session.

Encourage students to get into groups of three to five. Make sure that each group has at least one Bible. Distribute copies of "The Ins and Outs of Heaven" handout and writing utensils to each group. Give them sufficient time to work through the questions on the sheet. If particular questions arise during their study, refer to the information in the **Book Quakes**, **What's Up With That** and **Controversial Q and A** sections.

After groups have completed their work, say, **"It is impossible for us to imagine the immensity of all that will take place on that day when Christ comes riding on his white horse, victorious over sin and death forever. For those who have chosen to run away from God's presence in their lives, it will be an eternity of agony—but for the faithful of God, especially for those who have lost their lives for the cause of Christ, what a day of incredible joy!"**

Materials needed:
Bibles; reproducible student sheet on page 52 of this book; writing utensils

IS THE SECOND COMING OF CHRIST THE SAME AS THE "RAPTURE"?

It depends on whom you ask! The word "rapture" is not used in the Bible; it is derived from the Latin. The term means, "to snatch away" and refers to the catching away of believers before the world comes to an end (see 1 Thessalonians 4:16, 17; 1 Corinthians 15:50-57). The second coming of Christ is mentioned in 23 of the 27 New Testament books in the Bible. There are over 300 references! In Revelation, Jesus says, "I come quickly" seven times. The New Testament is clear that the return of Christ is a literal, physical reality.

There are many differing views on the timing of Christ's return. First Corinthians 15:51 refers to Christ's return as a "wonderful secret" in which "not all of us will die, but we will all be transformed." Those who anticipate a "rapture" believe that Christians who are alive at the time will supernaturally be taken up to Heaven without facing death. Those who are convinced that Christ's second coming and the rapture are two separate events also have different perspectives:

1. Christians will be raptured (taken up) *before* the seven-year tribulation.
2. Believers will be raptured *in the middle of* the seven-year tribulation period.
3. The rapture will occur *at the end of* the tribulation just before the second coming.
4. Extremely dedicated believers will be raptured *before* the tribulation, but the rest of the Christians will have to *go through* the tribulation.
5. The rapture will happen *at the height of* the frenzy of the tribulation (during the seventh seal).

Those who are proponents of the two distinct events view them this way:

Rapture	Second Coming
Jesus comes in the air	Jesus comes to earth
Comes in a moment	Happens with several signs
Jesus comes *for* his people	Jesus comes *with* his people
Tribulation now is underway	Tribulation begins at the millennium

It's extremely important *not* to argue with other people over these diverse views. We can agreeably disagree over these issues. Study God's Word to see if you can determine a particular doctrine, but do not be dogmatic wherever you "land." Some people have studied this subject for years and still have no concrete answers. At the same time, don't be afraid of Revelation. You are blessed as you read it!

AFTERSHOCKS

How Are People Really Judged?
- *Who judges humanity?* Jesus is the judge (John 5:27; 2 Timothy 4:1; Revelation 19:15, 16).
- *For what are we judged?* Our lifestyle (Ecclesiastes 12:14; Luke 12:2, 3; Revelation 20:12).
- *Who will be judged?* All humans (2 Corinthians 5:10; Revelation 20:11-13).
- *How will people be judged?* With perfect justice and fairness (Revelation 16:5-7; 19:11-13).

COSMIC CLOSURES

END-TIMES GAME SHOW

Create a game show similar to "Jeopardy," "Who Wants to be a Millionaire?" or "The Weakest Link." You can make the "set" as simple or as elaborate as you want. Choose two contestants to play. You can use either true or false or multiple-choice questions or have your contestants give their answers in the form of a question. Assign a point value to each question and ask for a student to keep score. Frame the following questions to fit your own style. The answers to each question are listed in parentheses.

1. What do all the angels and residents of Heaven spend their time doing? *(Worshiping God.)*
2. How will Jesus take decisive action to resolve the world conflict? *(He's provided eternal life for those who will freely come.)*
3. What is mankind's greatest problem? *(Sin.)*

Materials needed:
Props such as a microphone, podium and scoreboard; prizes

4. Why is sin the biggest problem? *(It leads to death.)*

5. Why should we be concerned with sin? *(It separates us from God.)*

6. What did Jesus do to solve the "sin" problem? *(He died on the cross and solved it permanently.)*

7. What will be the greatest defeat of all time? *(Death.)*

8. Who is our greatest enemy? *(Satan.)*

9. Why should people be concerned with Satan? *(He is a destroyer.)*

10. What is the eventual destiny for Satan? *(He will be thrown into the lake of fire.)*

11. Why are some people worried about dying? *(They fear the unknown.)*

12. Who will judge mankind? *(Jesus Christ is the judge.)*

13. Where will this judgment take place? *(Around God's great white throne.)*

14. How do I get my name in the Book of Life? *(By placing your faith in the Lamb of God, who is Jesus Christ.)*

15. If you were to die tonight, where would you spend eternity? *(Let them answer without any hints.)*

As you conclude this game show, question 15 should be restated. That question is left open-ended for the contestant to answer personally. As the "host" of the show, give a final plea for the students to make sure they know where they are going. Give a prize to each contestant. Close this session by thanking God that even though we have all sinned and fallen short of God's expectations for us, we will win in the end because Jesus "evened the score" for us by dying on the cross. It is his blood that wipes the slate clean.

II LIFE . . . AND DEATH . . . IN THE MOVIES

Show a clip from the movie, *Ghost* that runs from 1:55:06 to 2:00:56. In this scene, Carl's spirit (played by Tony Goldwyn) is taken to Hell by dark spirits and Sam (Patrick Swayze) is given the opportunity to say good-bye to his girlfriend before heading into the light of Heaven.

Ask a student to read Ephesians 2:8, 9 aloud. Then, close by saying something like this: **"Our good works don't get our names written down in the Lamb's Book of Life; only our faith and acceptance of God's gracious favor will do that. God extends the invitation. It is simply our gift to receive. Replay your life up to this point. Has there ever been a time when you accepted his grace as a payment for your sins? Have you accepted the rider of the white horse (who wears a robe dipped in blood) into your life? Can you call him your 'King of kings and Lord of lords'? Are you sure that there will be no second death for you?"**

Close in prayer, and follow up with any students who may need to talk with you further concerning the last question.

CAN I GET AN AMEN!
HALLELUJAH!?

Characters:
Narrator
Hallelujah chorus: two to ten people
Twenty-four elders: one person with a sign reading, "24 elders"
Four living creatures: one person with a sign reading, "Four living creatures"
God: one person
Angel: one person dressed like an angel
White horse: one person
Rider of the horse: one person
Vultures: two people
Beast: one person
False prophet: one person
The nations: one to three people

Narrator: After this, I heard the sound of a vast crowd in heaven shouting . . .

Hallelujah chorus: Hallelujah!

One chorus member: Salvation is from our God. Glory and power belong to him alone. His judgments are just and true. He has punished the great prostitute who corrupted the earth with her immorality, and he has avenged the murder of his servants.

Hallelujah chorus: *(sing in unison)* Hallelujah!

One chorus member: The smoke from that city ascends forever and forever!

Narrator: Then the twenty-four elders and the four living beings fell down . . . *(pause)* and worshiped God, who was sitting on the throne. The Hallelujah chorus cried out . . .

Hallelujah chorus: Amen! Hallelujah!

Narrator: And from the throne of God came a voice that said . . .

God: Praise our God, all his servants, from the least to the greatest, all who fear him.

Narrator: Then I heard again what sounded like the shout of a huge crowd, or the roar of mighty ocean waves, or the crash of loud thunder.

Hallelujah chorus: Hallelujah! For the Lord our God, the Almighty, reigns.

One chorus member: Let us be glad and rejoice and honor him. For the time has come for the wedding feast of the Lamb, and his bride has prepared herself. She is permitted to wear the finest white linen. (Fine linen represents the good deeds done by the people of God.)

Narrator: And the angel said,

Angel: Write this: Blessed are those who are invited to the wedding feast of the Lamb. These are true words that come from God.

Narrator: Then I fell down at his feet to worship him, but he said . . .

Angel: No, don't worship me. For I am a servant of God, just like you and other brothers and sisters who testify of their faith in Jesus. Worship God. For the essence of prophecy is to give a clear witness for Jesus.

Narrator: Then I saw heaven opened, and a white horse was standing there. And the one sitting on the horse was named Faithful and True. For he judges fairly and then goes to war. His eyes were bright like flames of fire, and on his head were many crowns. A name was written on him, and only he knew what it meant. He was clothed with a robe dipped in blood, and his title was the Word of God. The armies of heaven, dressed in pure white linen, followed him on white horses. *(Turn and say to the audience, "Use your imagination on this next one.")* From his mouth came a sharp sword, and with it he struck down the nations.

(The nations fall down.)

He ruled them with an iron rod, and he trod the winepress of the fierce wrath of almighty God. On his robe and thigh was written this title: King of kings and Lord of lords. Then I saw an angel standing in the sun, shouting to the vultures flying high in the sky . . .

Angel: Come! Gather together for the great banquet God has prepared. Come and eat the flesh of kings, captains, and strong warriors; of horses and their riders; and of all humanity, both free and slave, small and great.

Narrator: Then I saw the beast gathering the kings of the earth and their armies in order to fight against the one sitting on the horse and his army. And the beast was captured, and with him the false prophet who did mighty miracles on behalf of the beast—miracles that deceived all who had accepted the mark of the beast and who worshiped his statue. Both the beast and his false prophet were thrown alive into the lake of fire that burns with sulfur. Their entire army was killed by the sharp sword that came out of the mouth of the one riding the white horse. And all the vultures of the sky gorged themselves on the dead bodies.

The INS AND OUTS OF HEAVEN

According to Revelation 19:1-8, why is Heaven joyful?

In this chapter, we see a rider on a white horse. Who is this great warrior and what are some of his names?

What is the marriage of the Lamb? (Revelation 19:7-9)

In Revelation 19:15, the rider has a sharp sword come from his mouth. What do you think this sword is?
(See Ephesians 6:17.)

Based on Hebrews 4:12, what is the purpose of the sword?

In your own words describe the scenario in Revelation 19:17-21.

Satan will be locked in the bottomless pit for a thousand years, being unable to deceive the nations (Revelation 20:3).
What do you think life on earth might be like during that time?

How do you think Satan might deceive people into taking the mark of the beast? (Revelation 20:4)

After Satan is released from the bottomless pit, he will be allowed to roam the earth for a short time (Revelation 20:7, 8).
What do you think life will be like during that time?

Based on 2 Corinthians 5:10, who will appear before God in the final judgment at his white throne?

How can we be assured that our names will be written in the "Book of Life"? (See Revelation 20:11-15 and Romans 10:9.)

PICTURES FROM HEAVEN

John provides a vision of what is yet to come—he is allowed to peak into Heaven itself and behold its magnificence. And, John's words answer all of the burning questions most people have about it: What will Heaven be like? What will we be doing there? How big is Heaven? Will we know each other there? Are there rewards in Heaven? What will our bodies be like? Then, he encounters the risen Jesus who extends an invitation for all to come into his presence for eternity—for he is coming soon!

OPENING SHAKES

I VIRTUAL AFTERLIFE

Before your meeting, take a "film crew" out to interview some teenagers. Ask any or all of the following questions:
  • **What happens when you die?**
  • **Do you think Heaven exists? If so, what is it like?**
  • **Do you think Hell is a real place? If so, what is it like?**
  • **If you believe in the afterlife, what do you expect to happen to you?**

After you've done your filming, put your presentation together and have it prepared to show to students.

After all students have arrived, begin this activity by asking, **"Have you ever wondered what other people believe about Heaven? Well, we went out on the streets and asked people what they thought. I'd like you to hear what they said."**

Play the tape for students. When the tape is over, debrief with these questions:
  • **What surprised you about their responses?**
  • **If I had asked you these same questions, how might you have responded?**
  • **Why don't some people believe in Heaven or Hell?**
  • **Do you have to believe in Heaven or Hell to be saved? Explain.**

Conclude by saying something like this: **"Today we're going to learn what Revelation says about Heaven. We'll see that Heaven is a real place, and anyone can go there."**

II HOLLYWOOD RANTS ON THE AFTERLIFE

Before the session, gather a few video clips from different movies that mention or describe Heaven. If you're stumped on what movies to show, there's a list in the sidebar on page 54 that will get you started.

Begin by asking, **"What does Hollywood say about the afterlife? Let's look at several different movie clips and ask the question,**

LESSON TEXT
Revelation 21:1–22:21

LESSON FOCUS
Heaven is described as "the holy city," a perfect place of eternal reward for those who have remained faithful to the Lamb.

LESSON GOALS
As a result of participating in this session, students will:
• Get a clue about what the afterlife will be like.
• Understand the meaning of some images of Heaven and Hell.
• Prepare for Christ's return.

Materials needed:
Video camera; blank videotape; TV and VCR

Materials needed:
Videotapes; TV and VCR

Try one or more of these videos for this opener:

• *Heaven Can Wait* (1978). Warren Beatty is about to be killed and an angel takes him to a "weigh station." The clip starts at 9:39 and ends at 12:45 with the statement, "This is what comes after life and after dreams."

• *Down to Earth* (2001). This movie is a spin-off of *Heaven Can Wait*. The clip begins at 6:50 with Chris Rock getting hit by a truck and ends at 9:40 when Rock realizes he is in Heaven, but was mistakenly taken too soon by an angel.

• *K-PAX* (2001). Kevin Spacey is Prot, who says he's from a planet called K-PAX. Prot is placed in a psychiatric unit for supervision by Jeff Bridges. Although this is not a reference to the afterlife, what Prot describes about his life on K-PAX has many similarities to the biblical narrative of Heaven. No marriages, no families, just each person caring for one another and knowing right from wrong. The scene starts at 23:18 with the opening line, "This is so much better. It's a lot like home" and ends at 26:00 with the line, "You humans, sometimes it's hard to imagine how you've made it this far." (See **Controversial Q and A** on page 56.)

• *Little Nicky* (2000). This absurd movie depicts Adam Sandler as the devil's son. Begin with the scene early in the movie, at 3:38, where Sandler is told that his dad, the devil, might retire as the prince of darkness. End the clip at 5:22 in which Sandler's two brothers discuss how they want to take over the reins of Hell.

To learn more about what Heaven is like, pick up Anne Graham Lotz's book, *Heaven My Father's House* ("W" Publishing, a Division of Thomas Nelson, © 2001). It is a neat little book with insights on Heaven.

'How accurate is Hollywood's portrayal of the afterlife?'"

Choose several of the films listed that will provoke students to discover what Hollywood thinks about Heaven. Show the clips to students. After you have viewed them, lead your students in a discussion about what impressions the clips left on them. Ask questions like:

• **How realistic was their portrayal of Heaven and Hell?**

• **Does this fit your image of what Heaven will be like?**

• **What are some things that struck you the most from these clips?**

• **Do you think Heaven exists? If so, what is it like?**

• **Do you think Hell is a real place? If so, what is it like?**

If you don't have access to video editing equipment, ask the debriefing questions as tapes are being changed.

Close by saying, **"Let's see what the end of the Bible has to say on this subject."**

BOOK QUAKES

REVELATION 21:1-9

The apostle John is treated to a magnificent vision of the future home of God's people. The entire world will be destroyed and recreated into a "new heaven and a new earth." The old earth and the sea are no more. The "new Jerusalem" is described as "the holy city." The imagery of this city is in agreement with Ephesians 5, which describes the church as a bride. The people of God are the new Jerusalem. Resembling a bride, Christians are preparing for their bridegroom, Jesus Christ.

God's presence is everywhere and evil is nowhere to be found. Images such as giving "springs of the water of life" suggest that all spiritual needs will be met. And look at the list of things that are noticeably absent—no sadness, no crying, no problems and no pain!

21:10-22

John has a vision of the awesome city that is full of God's glory. The city's measurements are a perfect cube, about 1,400 miles wide and high (that's about the distance between New York and Houston). God has built something with plenty of room. John's description of Heaven includes all kinds of symbolism. Here's a list of some of the images he paints:

• The twelve gates, each made from a single pearl, speak of access into Heaven.

• The twelve foundation stones, inlaid with twelve precious gems, speak of Heaven's symmetry.

• The street of pure gold, as clear as glass, speaks of purity.

• God's throne speaks of God's reign.

• The river running through the city speaks of restoration.

• No temple exists because the Lord is the splendor.

21:23–22:5

Since the Lamb is the light, there's no need for any other source of light. It is hard to comprehend, but in comparing the brightness of the sun's rays, the Lord God will so brilliantly illuminate the city that there will be no night, no evil, no sun or moon. That is some brightness!

The last chapter of the Bible begins with John describing an awesome river filled with the water of life, clear as crystal and flowing directly from the throne of God—symbolizing that real life comes from his heart. The river winds down the main street, signifying that the life of God invades all of his people. All needs are met, all thirst will be quenched. God will be center stage. The ultimate thrill of Heaven will be to see God's face.

22:6-21

John is jolted back into "reality" with the powerful statement from Jesus in Revelation 22:7, "Look, I am coming soon! Blessed are those who obey the prophecy written in this scroll." John quotes Jesus three times in saying, "I am coming soon" (vv. 7, 12, 20). Jesus says he will repay everyone according to what he has done. This final chapter is a wrap-up of the blessedness of Heaven and those invited. The invitation is to "Come." All who are thirsty should answer his invitation to come and freely drink from the water of life.

WHAT'S UP WITH THAT?

ARE HEAVEN AND HELL LITERAL OR SYMBOLIC PLACES?

Heaven is mentioned over 500 times in the Bible. Those who claim that Heaven is a literal place quote Jesus in John 14:1-3 when he referred to "my Father's home" and then said, "I am going to prepare a place for you." The apostle Paul spoke of visiting the third heaven (2 Corinthians 12:2) and Hebrews 11:16 refers to Heaven as a city. Those who say "Heaven" is symbolic point to Revelation 21 and 22, suggesting that a literal place with walls, gates and gold streets is purely illustrative.

Jesus spoke of Hell more than anyone else in the New Testament. Different scholars have used Luke 16:19-31 to "prove" both a literal and a symbolic interpretation of Hell. Literalists believe that Hell is a place of torment, memory, fire, pain and separation from God. Some scholars believe that Hell is a real place but the "fire and brimstone" is only imagery. Others suggest that a self-absorbed life is comparable to a living "Hell."

There are a variety of Greek words used to describe Hell. The phrase "bottomless pit" is used in Revelation 20:1-3 to describe the place where Satan will be bound for the millennium. Luke 16:23 and Revelation 1:18 refer to "Hades" as a place where the lost are held until the final judgment. "Gehenna" is the word most often used in the Bible for Hell, considered a place of torment for Satan, his fallen angels and the lost (Revelation 20:10, 14, 15).

Some believe that Hell is a place of eternal suffering, and others contend that Hell is a place of annihilation (no pain or suffering; the lost are eliminated). One thing is for sure. We have the chance to be in the presence of Jesus 24/7. Who would be opposed to that?

TEACHING TREMORS

I GRASPING THE AFTERLIFE

Before the session begins, make photocopies of the "Life after Life" handout on page 58. Have your students break into small groups of three to five and give each group a photocopy of the handout and something to write with. Ask students to write down their thoughts about what Heaven and Hell will be like.

After you have given them enough time to do so, ask groups to share some of the things they came up with. Draw a vertical line down

Materials needed:
Reproducible student sheet on page 58 of this book; writing utensils; Bible; markerboard or poster board; marker

Materials needed:
Reproducible student sheet on page 59 of this book; writing utensils; Bibles

the middle of your board. On the left side at the top write the title, "Pictures of Heaven" and on the right side at the top write the title, "Pictures of Hell." As students share their responses to the questions on the handout, record their thoughts on the appropriate side of the board. After all groups have had an opportunity to share, compare what they said to some of the descriptions of Heaven and Hell found in Revelation 21, 22. Refer to the information in the **Book Quakes** section as you have need.

Ask students, **"How often have you wondered about what happens after you die?"** (See how they respond to that question.)

Conclude by saying, **"One of the great mysteries is what the afterlife is really like. It's perfectly clear in God's Word that we will be held accountable for our actions and spend eternity *with* him or separated *from* him, but what does that look like? God gives us a small glimpse in the last two chapters of the Bible."**

A SNEAK PREVIEW OF THE AFTER-LIFE

Before the session begins, make photocopies of the student sheet on page 59. Have students get in small groups, making sure that you have at least five groups. A group can consist of one or two students. Make sure each group has at least one Bible. Distribute copies of the handout on page 59 and writing utensils to each group. You may want to have on hand different versions and a few modern paraphrases of the Bible (such as *The Message*) for their study. Comment, **"Let's take a look at what Revelation says about our final destination."**

Assign groups to research one of the Scripture passages on the handout, and answer the questions pertaining to their text. Then, ask groups to report to the entire group what they found in their passage. As they share, students can fill in the rest of the handout. After each group has responded, discuss some of the following questions:

• **"Do you think these are literal descriptions of Heaven, or do you think John was describing Heaven in words that we could understand?"**

• **"How can we make a reservation for this eternal destination?"**

• **"How do you think the apostle John felt after being permitted to look into Heaven?"**

CONTROVERSIAL Q AND A

WILL THERE BE FAMILY RELATIONSHIPS IN HEAVEN?

Jesus said in Matthew 22:30, "For when the dead rise, they won't be married. They will be like the angels in heaven." Evidently there will be no marriage in Heaven, for we will be like the angels. What does that mean? Angels were sex-less. In other words, there will be no need for marriage or the expression of sexual intimacy in Heaven. All the intimacy we will need will be fulfilled, just by being in the presence of God! There will be male and female in Heaven, but apparently no sexual relations with one another.

Will we know family members and friends? The Bible seems to indicate that we will intimately know one another. First Corinthians 13:10 speaks of when the "end comes" we will "see everything with perfect clarity" and will "know everything completely, just as God knows me now" (v. 12). We will have total understanding about all of life and its mysteries. Jesus told the story of the rich man recognizing Lazarus in Heaven (Luke 16:19-31). Apparently, we will have complete understanding in Heaven.

COSMIC CLOSURES

I | PERSONAL WORSHIP

Ahead of time collect some of your students' favorite worship songs on CD or DVD. You'll also need to write the following words on transparencies or in a PowerPoint® presentation: "My Sin," "Crucified" and "Forever."

Begin this activity by saying, **"Through today's study we've learned a lot about the end of our lives. We have the opportunity to choose where we go when we die, and I'd like you to consider where you plan on going when your life on earth is over."**

Ask students to find a place in the room where they can feel alone. Play the songs and show the words on the wall one at a time using an overhead projector or PowerPoint® presentation. Instruct students that as they see each word displayed, they need to consider the meaning of each word.

After the last song is over, say something like this: **"God offers us forgiveness for the wrong things we've done. Without his forgiveness, we won't be able to enter his presence and worship him forever. I'd like you to consider your sins, and the things that prevent you from walking intimately with God. What do you need to say to him?"**

Close this session by allowing students to spend some time in silent prayer with God, talking with him about whatever he has just laid on their hearts.

Materials needed:
Worship songs; CD or DVD player; transparency and overhead projector or PowerPoint® presentation and screen

II | FUNERAL DROP

Before the meeting, either rent a casket from a funeral home or purchase a cardboard box that could be used as a casket. Distribute index cards and writing utensils to students, and ask them to write the following statement on their card: **"I surrender my sins. I know the only way to Heaven is to have the hope of eternal life through Jesus. I receive his forgiveness."**

Encourage students to write some of their sins on the card if they want to. After they have finished writing, instruct students to put their cards in the coffin. After all students have placed their cards, invite a few of them to serve as pallbearers, and carry the coffin outside and leave it behind the church. Invite your entire group to follow the pallbearers. When everyone is outside, and the coffin procession has been completed, invite a few students to close your session with a word of prayer, thanking God for his forgiveness, and the opportunity to live forever with him.

Materials needed:
Casket; 3" x 5" index cards; writing utensils

Life after Life

PICTURES OF HEAVEN

- What do you think Heaven will look like?

- What do you think we will do in Heaven?

- Who do you think you will see in Heaven?

- What do you think Heaven will feel like?

PICTURES OF HELL

- What do you think Hell will look like?

- What do you think people will do in Hell?

- Who do you think will be in Hell?

- What do you think Hell will feel like?

SNEAK PREVIEW
of the After-Life

TAKE ONE: Revelation 21:1-8

• What do you learn about the "new Jerusalem"?

• Who is welcome there?

• Who is not welcome there?

TAKE TWO: Revelation 21:12-17

• What is present in the city?

• Why would there be walls in the city?

TAKE THREE: Revelation 21:18-27

• Why is there no temple in the new city?

• Why does this city have gates like gems?

• Why is the city filled with images of light?

TAKE FOUR: Revelation 22:1-10

• What is happening in the city?

• What is the meaning of the imagery of God's "name written" on our foreheads?

TAKE FIVE: Revelation 22:11-21

• Why do you think Jesus is coming back?

• What do the names Alpha, Omega, First and Last say about the nature of Jesus?

• Who is left outside of the new Jerusalem?

• Based on Revelation 22:17, who is welcome in the new city?

DOES GOD HOLD TO AN END-TIME VIEW?
A PANEL DISCUSSION

Interest in exploring eschatology (end times study) is on the rise, as evidenced by all the books, both fiction and non-fiction, that have been written. The *Left Behind* series continues to rank high on the *New York Times* Bestseller list. Many well-meaning Christians have opposing views on the end times. What all Bible-believing Christians do believe is that Christ will come back again. The differences primarily concern the timing, the sequence of events and all the details surrounding his coming.

Essentially, this session is a panel discussion. What will you need in order to make this as practical for your students as possible?

A FACILITATOR

Consider the youth pastor as the facilitator, since he understands teens. You want someone who can *guide*, not *control* the discussion. The hard line to tow is not letting the time get so theologically heavy that students "check out " intellectually and emotionally. Be sensitive to their attention spans. You may want to photocopy all of the **What's Up With That?** and **Controversial Q and A** sections from the six sessions in this book. They will provide some excellent background information for the facilitator without overwhelming him or her.

TIME WARNINGS

Panel discussions can be electrifying or boring! Plan on going 30 to 40 minutes, no more. Consider writing some questions on 3" x 5" index cards that your students could ask to keep them interested!

PANEL

Invite people with differing perspectives on end times. Before you recruit them, review the material in the **What's Up With That?** and **Controversial Q and A** sections in session 5 that deal with these varying perspectives. If possible, find engaging men and women who hold these different views:

- *Pre-tribulation*
This view holds that the rapture will happen before the tribulation.

- *Mid-tribulation*
This position states that the rapture will happen in the middle of the tribulation (3 1/2 years).

- *Postmillennial*
This perspective believes that Christ will come after the millennium.

- *Amillennial*
Most Roman Catholics are amillennialists, believing that we are living in the kingdom now.

FOCUS
Throughout the course of this study, many different viewpoints have been presented concerning a number of issues in the book. This event will give your students an opportunity to further discuss some of the various interpretations of Revelation.

GOALS
As a result of participating in this event, students will:
- Learn to think critically concerning the end times.
- Understand that there is no "one-size-fits-all" theology for the end times.
- Engage one another on a deeper level.

TOP 10 QUESTIONS

Here are some possible questions for your panel. Encourage participants to be simple, short and clear with their answers. Each answer should be 30 seconds to two minutes. Long-winded responses simply won't work! Your panel can take a free-for-all-talk-when-you-want approach like some of television's talk shows, or you can keep it orderly by having the facilitator moderate the discussion by calling on different panel members to answer certain questions.

1. Do you believe we are living in the end times?
2. What are the signs of Christ's coming?
3. Do you believe Christ will return soon?
4. What is your view of the rapture?
5. What is your view of the millennium?
6. What is your view of the antichrist?
7. What do you believe about the return of Christ?
8. Do you believe in a tribulation period? If yes, what will it be like?
9. Do you believe in a literal Heaven and Hell? Or are they symbolic of something else?
10. What will people be doing in Heaven?

BOUNDARIES

Involve your panel to "balance the ledger"—in other words, do not let some panelists "hog" the floor while the more introverted tend to shy away from heated discussions. Make sure that each panelist gets equal time to speak his or her mind. Call on a particular panelist by name if he has not contributed to a given subject.

CLOSING

Do not feel that you have to get through all the information. No matter what you do, your teens will not leave the meeting with eschatology all figured out. In summary, in his book *When Christ Comes*, Max Lucado expresses the best attitude in approaching the end times, "For the Christian, the return of Christ is not a riddle to be solved or a code to be broken, but rather a day to be anticipated." Thank everyone for coming. Make sure you give your panel members some type of thank-you gift!

RESOURCES FOR REVELATION

101 Answers to the Most Asked Questions About The End Times, by Mark Hitchcock (Sisters, OR: Multnomah, 2001).

Be Victorious. New Testament Study in Revelation, by Warren W. Wiersbe (Colorado Springs, CO: Chariot Victor, 1985).

Charts of Christian Theology and Doctrine, by Wayne House (Grand Rapids, MI: Zondervan Publishing House, 1992).

A Commentary on the Revelation of John, by George Eldon Ladd (Grand Rapids, MI: Wm. B. Eerdmans Publishing, 1972).

E-Quake: Unlocking the Book of Revelation, by Jack Hayford (Nashville, TN: Thomas Nelson Publishers, 1999).

Revelation: Holy Living in an Unholy World, by Bob Mulholland (Grand Rapids, MI: Francis Asbury Press, 1990).

The Revelation Letters: Preparing Youth Groups for Christ's Return, by David Olshine (Cincinnati, OH: Standard Publishing, 2001).

The Revelation of John, vol. 1, 2, by William Barclay (Philadelphia, PA: Westminster Press, 1976).

The Revelation of St. John, by Leon Morris (Grand Rapids, MI: Wm. B. Eerdmans Publishing, 1978).

Revelation: The Christian's Ultimate Victory, by John MacArthur (Nashville, TN: Word Publishing, 2001).

Revelation: Unlocking the Mysteries With Youth, by Samuel Parvin (Nashville, TN: Abingdon Press, 1999).

When Christ Comes, by Max Lucado (Nashville, TN: Word Publishing, 1999).

ABOUT THE AUTHOR

Dr. David Olshine chairs the youth ministries program at Columbia International University in Columbia, South Carolina. David has authored 19 books, including *The Revelation Letters*, *Actual Reality* and *How to Have Real Conversation With Your Teen*. Annually, he speaks to thousands of teens, parents of teens and youth workers. David and his wife, Rhonda, are the parents of Rachel and Andrew.

CONTRIBUTORS

Joshua Treece studied youth ministry and graduated from Columbia International University (C. I. U.). He helped with sessions one, two and six.

Christy Herge has a master's degree in education from C. I. U. She contributed to sessions three and four.

David Saine is youth pastor at Kingsland United Methodist Church. He contributed to session five.

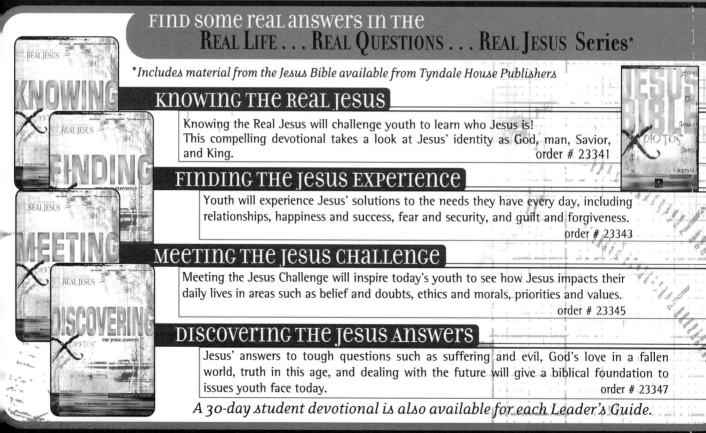